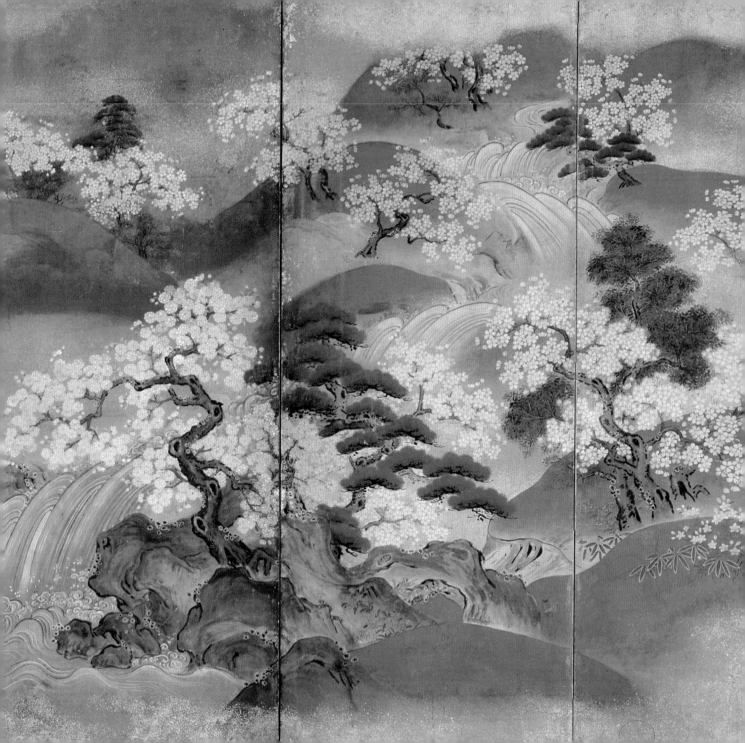

BEHIND
GOLDEN
SCREENS

TREASURES FROM THE
TOKYO FUJI ART MUSEUM

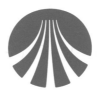

A catalogue of the exhibition held in
the Royal Museum of Scotland Edinburgh
from 10 August to 20 October 1991

NATIONAL MUSEUMS OF SCOTLAND 1991

Outside Covers: Grape Arbour. Detail of a pair of six-fold screens by a member of the Kanō School. The golden vine leaves, clouds and stream are distinguished by different patterns. (No 3)

Frontispiece: Cherry blossoms on the banks of the Tatsuta river. Detail from the righthand folding screen of a pair showing Spring and Autumn. A detail from the lefthand screen, showing Autumn maples on the Yoshino mountains, is illustrated on page 131. Japanese read screens from right to left. (No 14)

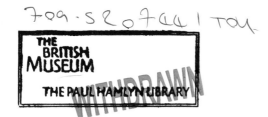
Published by the National Museums of Scotland, Chambers Street, Edinburgh EH1 1JF

Edited and designed by the Publications Office, National Museums of Scotland
Typeset and printed by Alna Press, Broxburn, West Lothian

British Library Cataloguing in Publication Data
A catalogue record for this book is available from the British Library
ISBN 0 948636 28 9

Contents

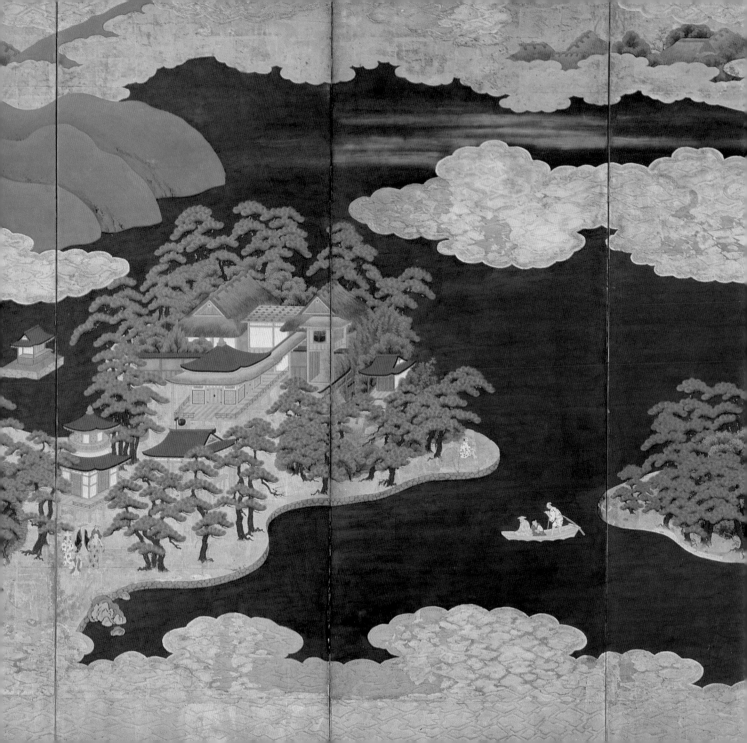

Prefaces

As a founder, I am delighted that the Tokyo Fuji Art Museum is able to offer the exhibition 'Behind Golden Screens' from its collection, to introduce Japanese art to the public at the Royal Museum of Scotland. This is particularly significant as Edinburgh, the capital city of Scotland, has a proud cultural history of its own, adorned as it is with its great castle and beautiful natural surroundings. It has also been the birthplace of many important people in the field of the Arts, including Sir Walter Scott, the great writer of the romantic period.

This exhibition is one of the official events in The Japan Festival commemorating the hundredth anniversary of The Japan Society, which has been actively promoting exchanges of friendship and goodwill between our two countries. It is also one of the major events in the Edinburgh International Festival, the 'Olympiad of Arts'. The exhibition features some 120 selected masterpieces, which represent the flower of our collection of Japanese art.

As is commonly known, Japanese art has been greatly influenced by Asian continental culture, particularly that of China. With this as a background, Japan's characteristic cultural taste and view of nature has brought forth many masterpieces. The Muromachi, Momoyama and Edo periods (fourteenth to nineteenth century) were the most productive in the history of Japanese art. During the times of samurai military rule, a variety of works resulted from factors such as contact with overseas cultures, remarkable economic progress, a revival of classical culture and the rise of a culture of the common people. Their outstanding beauty is reflected in paintings, craftsmanship and other artistic fields and through the ages their unique charm has captured people's hearts.

Amo no Hashidate, a sandbar in Western Japan, is one of the country's three most famous scenic spots. Travel was a popular pastime in the Edo period and this detail from a folding screen shows visitors taking boat rides to the Monju-Dō temple opposite the sandbar. (No 15)

I hope that the art treasures from these periods – which could be called the 'Japanese Renaissance' – will captivate the people of Scotland too, whether it is the splendour of the screen paintings, the colourfully drawn *ukiyo-e* prints, the design of the beautiful lacquer-ware, or the armour and swords created with the most elaborate technical skills.

I believe there is no more reliable way to realize mutual understanding, friendship and peace between the peoples of the world than through cultural exchange, because it can cross the boundaries of history, ethnic origin, climate and so on, and bring about understanding and tolerance.

Mutual exchange between the United Kingdom and Japan has a long history politically, economically and culturally, from the Edo period in the seventeenth century up to today. I sincerely hope that, based on such close ties, this exhibition will contribute to a deepening understanding of Japanese culture and encourage further cultural exchange programmes between our countries.

I wish this exhibition great success from the depths of my heart, and in doing so extend my profound gratitude to Sir Hugh Cortazzi, ex-Chairman of the British Japan Society, and to Dr Robert Anderson, Director of the National Museums of Scotland and the many others associated with the event and involved in its presentation, who have given us their generous support and help to make it possible.

Daisaku Ikeda
Founder
Tokyo Fuji Art Museum

It is with great pleasure that we welcome an exhibition from one of the most outstanding collections in Japan. 'Behind Golden Screens: Treasures from the Tokyo Fuji Art Museum' is a display of over one hundred objects never before shown in the United Kingdom, and it makes a most significant contribution to the Japan Festival in 1991. 'Behind Golden Screens' is also a feature of the Edinburgh International Festival at which Japanese performing art has been so well received in previous years.

Since the middle of the nineteenth century the National Museums of Scotland have acquired many Japanese objects, partly as a result of donations made by Scots who travelled to Japan and were captivated by the style and beauty of Japanese art. Yet some areas are not covered in Scottish collections and the opportunity to see screens and paintings for which Japan has such a justifiable reputation is a particular privilege.

The relationship between Scotland and Japan has developed and expanded over recent years, and this is reflected in the increasing number of Japanese visitors to the Museums. We are confident that this exhibition will contribute to better understanding between our two cultures and to fruitful co-operation in the future.

On behalf of the Trustees of the National Museums of Scotland I wish to thank all those in the Tokyo Fuji Art Museum who have done so much, and with so much generosity, to make it possible to bring this exhibition to Scotland.

The Marquess of Bute
Chairman, Board of Trustees
National Museums of Scotland

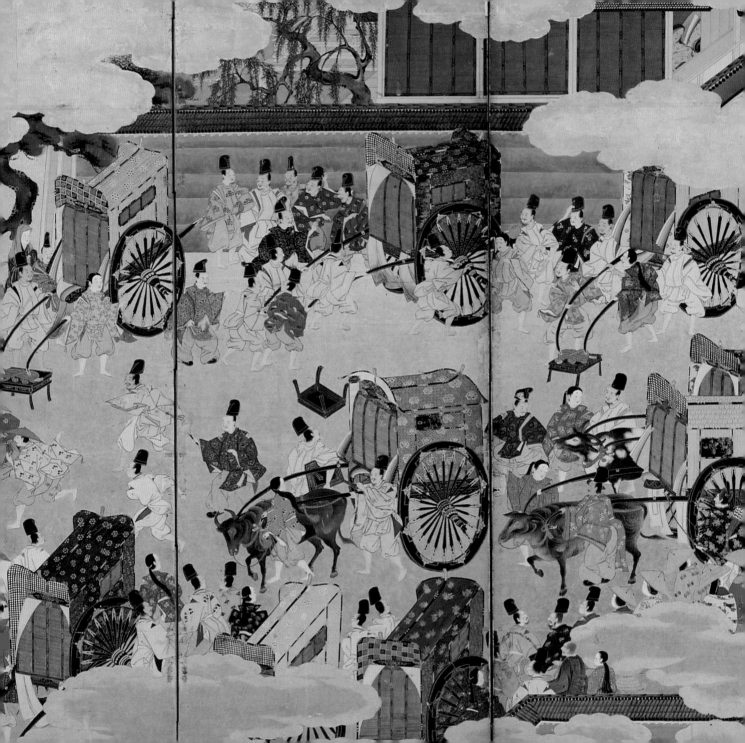

BEHIND GOLDEN SCREENS

Jane Wilkinson

The beautiful designs on Japanese screens were often painted in luminous colours against a gold background. Golden clouds were depicted drifting across the seasonal blooms of a mountainous landscape, or they separated views of life at court or scenes on the battlefield. Gold picks up light and these 'golden screens' helped to brighten the dark rooms and corridors of the palaces and castles of the wealthy in Japan.

Domestic architecture in Japan is a product of climate and raw materials. Although adapted to suit succeeding generations, many characteristics originated in the Heian period (794–1185). Sliding screens are integral to the structure of a traditional home. They divide the rooms and corridors, allowing the flexibility to alter the space to suit the need. In the humid summer the exterior screens can be opened to the beautiful gardens and allow movement of air through the building to prevent damp. The wooden verandahs become part of the room. Their overhanging eaves give shade from the direct heat of the midday sun. In winter the sun is lower in the sky. It warms the rooms on sunny days but when necessary layers of screens can be closed to keep out the winter storms.

There are several types of architectural screen, ranging from heavy wooden storm doors to a a variety, known as *shoji*, in which white, semi-translucent paper is stretched over a latticed wooden frame. Only one type of these sliding screens, *fusuma*, is represented in the exhibition. These were made of several layers of paper stretched over a light wooden framework. The last layer on which the design is painted is either paper or silk, as in the four *fusumas* painted by Susuki Kiitsu (1796–1858) (No 13).

These are a delightful example of the Japanese artist's dynamic use of the space provided by four adjacent sliding doors

In the *Tale of Gengi*, written in the 10th century, annual festivals were an opportunity for courtiers to show off their finery, illustrated in this detail from a pair of folding screens. (No 8)

between two rooms. The god of thunder Raijin appears with his drums amongst the thunder clouds on one side, whilst Fujin the wind god is seen on the reverse racing across the sky with his bag of winds. A similar design was painted in the middle of the seventeenth century by Tawaraya Sōtatsu on a pair of folding screens, now in the Kennin Temple, Kyoto. Kiitsu admired Sōtatsu's work and made use of the earlier design of 'Wind and Thunder Gods' on his sliding doors.

Folding screens were not built into the home. They could be folded up and stored easily until they were next needed. Their Japanese name, *byōbu*, is made up of two characters, *byō*, meaning fence or protection against, and *bu*, the wind. Sometimes they were used outside to form an enclosure, but more usually they were inside, to divide off temporary areas for sleeping or entertaining. Their design and gold background emphasized the status of the person giving audience or hosting the entertainment. The screens often flanked seats of honour or decorated dark corners of the audience hall.

Most of the screens in this exhibition are *byōbu*. Originating in China, where they had graduated to more general use by the Han Dynasty (296 BC–221 AD), they first arrived in Japan in 686 AD as a gift from the Silla Kingdom in Korea to the court at Kyoto. In Japan they were made in a variety of sizes to suit a specific function or the taste of the period. Usually a pair of six-fold screens measured between one-and-a-half to two metres high and about three-and-three-quarter metres wide. However, the number of folds as well as the size could vary.

The panels of a folding screen are joined together by taking strips of paper placed horizontally from the front of one panel to the back of the next, so producing hinges which were reversed on alternate strips going in the opposite direction. This enabled the painter to treat each panel as an uninterrupted part of the final composition. Screens are read from right to left. A pair of screens provides a large surface which is divided into three sections for the

Susuki Kiitsu's thunder god, Raijin, with his drums in a detail from the furthest right of four sliding doors. (No 13)

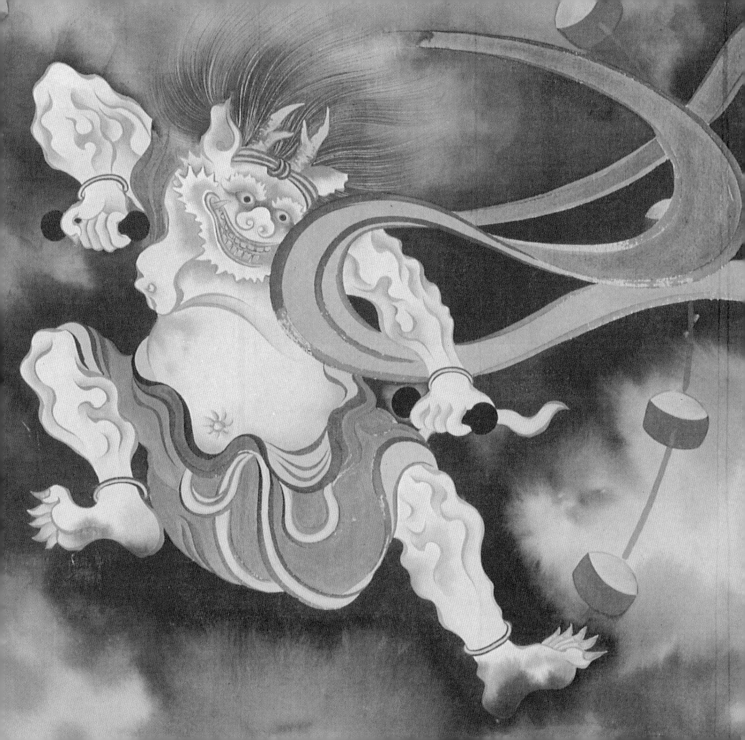

composition of the painting. The areas at the extreme left and right are viewed as if from close range, but the central area, occupying the adjoining halves of the two screens, is seen as if from a distance or from a bird's eye view.

This scheme is clearly seen in the pair of screens by Kanō Tsunenobu (1636–1713) of the four seasons (No 7). Spring is shown in a close-up view of a village with a river running through it on the far right. Summer and Autumn are distant views of the lake which occupies the adjoining halves of the two screens. Freshly fallen snow is painted on the umbrella of the figure crossing a bridge in the rocky landscape of Winter on the far left, again seen as if from close range. The perspective is vertical, that is as the eye moves up the picture the further away the objects appear.

Painting in Japan developed from Chinese models, but like so many aspects of Japanese culture the forms and ideas were absorbed and assimilated until a distinctive style evolved. This was true even among those artists continuing to use Chinese subjects and themes. Two parallel courses had developed by the sixteenth century when the earliest screens in the exhibition were painted: a purely Japanese style originating in the ninth century, and the brush and ink painting typical of the Zen school of Buddhist monks which picked up Chinese themes again in the fifteenth century.

Yamato-e, Japanese painting, had its origins in the Heian period (794–1185). The court at Kyoto lived a secluded life isolated from the ordinary people of the provinces. Having adopted Buddhism in the sixth century as part of a cultural package which included the Chinese writing system, methods of administration and architecture, three centuries later the Japanese court was in the process of finding its own identity. Painters turned with a new confidence to the world surrounding them. They depicted the four seasons and events associated with changes in the yearly cycle. Screens showing blossoms and visits to the shrines and festivals suitable to the time of year were often painted in sequence. Famous

Winter appears in the leftmost screen of the Four Seasons by Kanō Tsunenobu. (No 7)

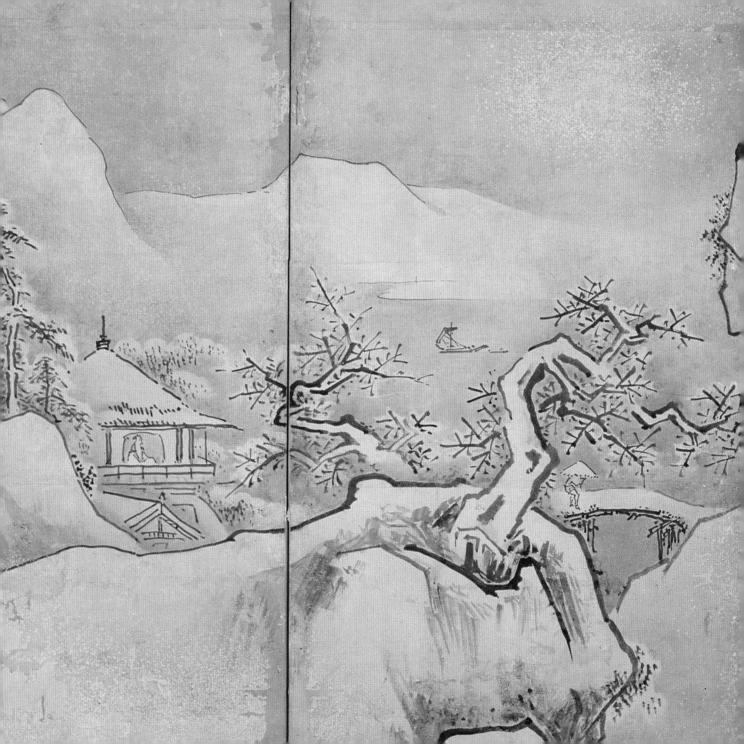

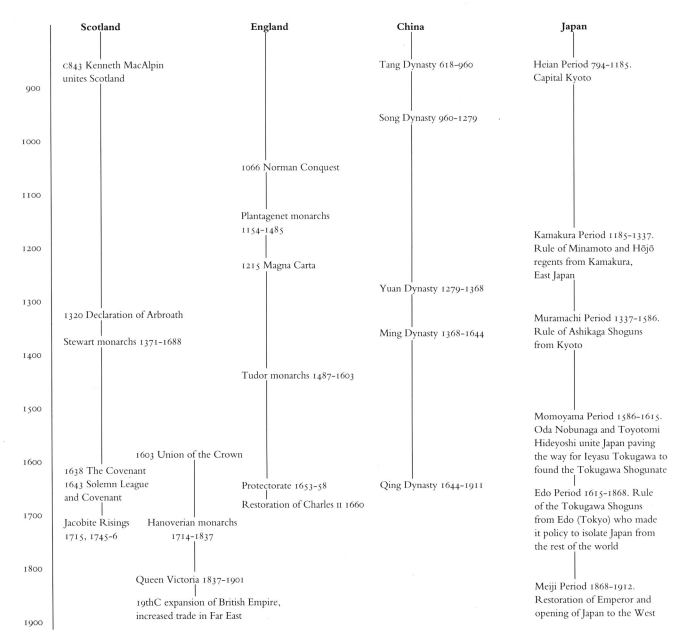

Scotland	England	China	Japan

Scotland

c.843 Kenneth MacAlpin unites Scotland

1320 Declaration of Arbroath

Stewart monarchs 1371-1688

1603 Union of the Crown

1638 The Covenant
1643 Solemn League and Covenant

Jacobite Risings 1715, 1745-6

England

1066 Norman Conquest

Plantagenet monarchs 1154-1485

1215 Magna Carta

Tudor monarchs 1487-1603

Protectorate 1653-58

Restoration of Charles II 1660

Hanoverian monarchs 1714-1837

Queen Victoria 1837-1901

19thC expansion of British Empire, increased trade in Far East

China

Tang Dynasty 618-960

Song Dynasty 960-1279

Yuan Dynasty 1279-1368

Ming Dynasty 1368-1644

Qing Dynasty 1644-1911

Japan

Heian Period 794-1185. Capital Kyoto

Kamakura Period 1185-1337. Rule of Minamoto and Hōjō regents from Kamakura, East Japan

Muramachi Period 1337-1586. Rule of Ashikaga Shoguns from Kyoto

Momoyama Period 1586-1615. Oda Nobunaga and Toyotomi Hideyoshi unite Japan paving the way for Ieyasu Tokugawa to found the Tokugawa Shogunate

Edo Period 1615-1868. Rule of the Tokugawa Shoguns from Edo (Tokyo) who made it policy to isolate Japan from the rest of the world

Meiji Period 1868-1912. Restoration of Emperor and opening of Japan to the West

900
1000
1100
1200
1300
1400
1500
1600
1700
1800
1900

places and beauty spots both outside and inside the capital were also popular subjects.

The first Japanese novel, the *Tale of Genji* , was written by a woman who was a lady-in-waiting at court. It evokes the elegance of life lived by the élite in Kyoto. She describes gatherings of courtiers and ladies to view the moon, play musical instruments, write poetry or picnic under the cherry blossom, all dressed in richly-coloured layers of silk. Prince Genji's many romantic assignations are always followed by the arrival of a poem alluding to the sad passing of the pleasures of the night before. This dreamlike existence is the source of Japanese classical themes in the art of later generations. The tale itself was often illustrated in pictorial scrolls.

Scenes from the *Tale of Genji* decorate a pair of screens painted in the Edo period (1615–1868) by an artist from the Tosa school (No 9). This school developed the *Yamato-e* style. The typical Japanese subject-matter found in Tosa painting is also seen in the two screens depicting famous battles from the *Heike Monogatari* (the *Historic Romance of the Taira Family*). The defeat of the Taira family by the Minamoto clan in 1185 marked the end of the Heian period. The new rulers established their headquarters on the east coast of Japan in Kamakura, a town quite close to modern Tokyo, far from the influence of the court at Kyoto.

Although the Kamakura period lasted only until 1337, it heralded two important factors for the future of Japanese political and economic history. The first of these was military rule which was to be the effective mode of government for the next seven hundred years. The second was the move away from Kyoto to the east of Japan. A stratagem, short-lived at this period, later ensured the success of the Tokugawa Shogunate in establishing their rule of Japan from Edo, modern Tokyo, for almost three hundred years.

The rise in power of the military families led to the development of new styles in painting. They wanted bold, colourful designs to decorate the interiors of their castles. Painted screens were needed to impress their power and wealth on visitors, whether friend or enemy. Kanō Eitoku (1543–90) was the fifth generation head of the Kanō family, a family of artists originating in the middle of the fifteenth century and continuing to the latter half of the nineteenth century. At first he followed the family tradition of monochrome ink painting in the Chinese style fashionable in the preceding period (No 1). However, he soon adapted his style to the needs of his powerful patrons. He was the first artist to use gold leaf as a background on which to paint, and his monumental style was copied by following generations. Blank areas of gold leaf were used to depict land, as in the design of Chinese phoenixes (No 12), or mist, as in the scenes of Mount Yoshino and the Tatsuta river (No 15), both painted by artists from the Kanō school.

Eitoku's style, using broad sweeping brushwork against a gold background, was eminently suited to the opulent decoration of the vast castles being built by Japan's leading military warlords of the Momoyama period (1586–1615) – men such as Toyotomi Hideyoshi (1537–98). He rose to power through the ranks of the samurai to become military leader of Japan, able to mount a successful invasion of Korea in 1592. He built Osaka castle, the largest and most splendid castle ever built, though unfortunately destroyed when the Toyotomis were overthrown in 1615. The gold clouds, stream and leaves of the vine on the screen depicting a grape arbour (No 3) are typical of this era. The gold has been raised from the surface of the painting using *gofun*, chalk powders, to differentiate leaves and clouds. Blank areas of gold are used to define the painting at the far extremes of the pair of screens.

Japan was finally united under Ieyasu Tokugawa, the first of the Tokugawa shoguns. He moved the seat of government to Edo, modern Tokyo, at the beginning of the seventeenth century. The Emperor was left in Kyoto, a ritual figurehead, though nominal head of state. Kyoto had suffered from more than a century of warfare and needed to rebuild. It was natural that new artistic values should develop in the old capital, the source of so much artistic heritage. The western provinces around Kyoto and Osaka were

The appearance of a phoenix was believed to herald a virtuous ruler, and was a favourite motif with Ieyasu Tokugawa who united Japan in 1615. (No 12, detail)

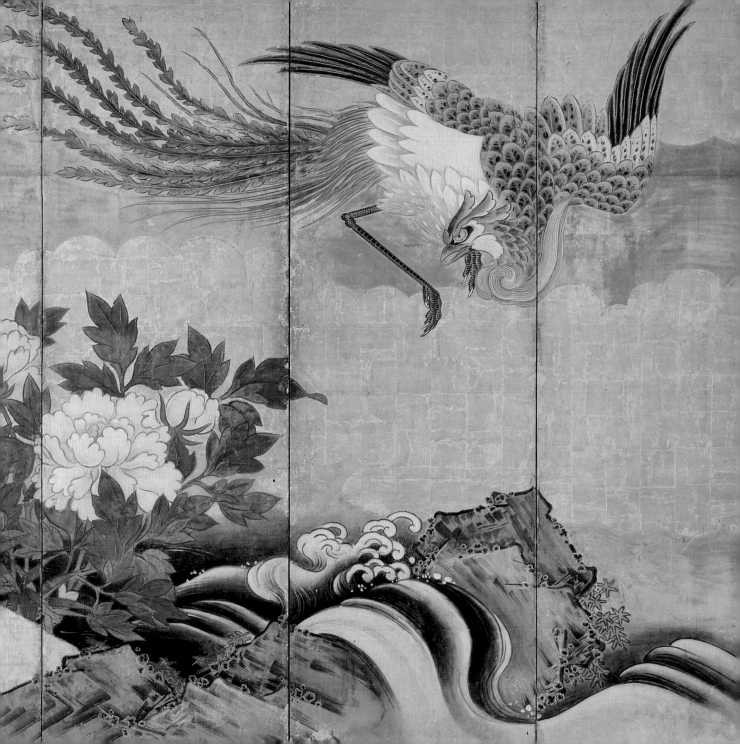

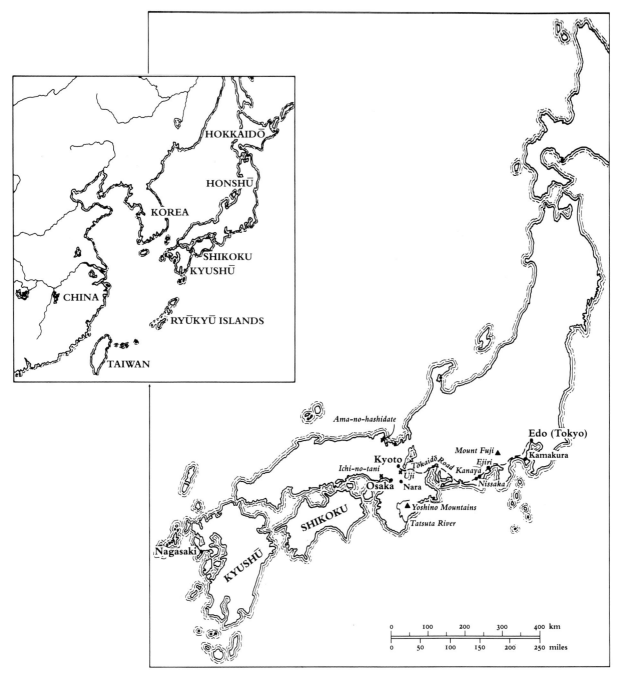

HOKKAIDŌ

HONSHŪ

KOREA

SHIKOKU
KYUSHŪ

CHINA

RYŪKYŪ ISLANDS

TAIWAN

Ama-no-hashidate

Edo (Tokyo)

Mount Fuji ▲
Kyoto   Kamakura
Ichi-no-tani   Tōkaidō Road
            Uji   Ejiri
                    Kanaya
         Nara   Nissaka
Osaka

          ▲ Yoshino Mountains
SHIKOKU
          Tatsuta River

Nagasaki

KYUSHŪ

0   100   200   300   400 km

0   50   100   150   200   250 miles

known as the Kansai. A Kansai style developed and continued to thrive throughout the Edo period (1615–1868). Even today there is a certain delicacy and beauty to be found in the lifestyle of Kyoto and Osaka citizens. Traditional values lay at the centre of this new movement but they were overlaid with a refinement and sophistication which was a reflection of the new age.

Artists such as Tawaraya Sōtatsu, who died in about 1640, epitomise the Rimpa school which blossomed amongst a colony of artists led by Hon'ami Kōetsu (1558–1637). Although the government wanted Kōetsu to move to Edo and serve as cultural adviser, they agreed to give him a large area of land lying to the north-east of Kyoto called Takagamine. Here, just outside Kyoto, artists were free to develop Kōetsu's theories. They included infusing classical Japanese taste into simple everyday affairs. Motifs were taken from the classical themes of the Heian period, and from nature, illustrating their common source. The resulting decorative style was a reaction against the flamboyant designs used boastfully by the military generals in their castles. The courtly traditions were reworked in a refined and stylish manner, as can be seen in the screen attributed to Sōtatsu (No 5). This artist is often called modern because of his composition. The bold design of pine trees and cherry blossoms pivots round the lower righthand corner, resembling the shape of a fan. It comes as no surprise to learn that he also designed fans.

At Takagamine Kōetsu gathered craftsmen around him who worked in many different media. He is associated with a group of lacquer objects. It is unlikely that he did more than supply designs for lacquerware during his lifetime, but his style was often copied long after his death, as can be seen in both a writing case and a box (Nos 44 and 54). Kōetsu also revived the classical style of calligraphy, producing a distinctive form of writing which was immediately recognizable as his own. He wrote *waka* poems of thirty-one syllables on papers often decorated by other members of his colony, for example Sōtatsu. These were put together as books

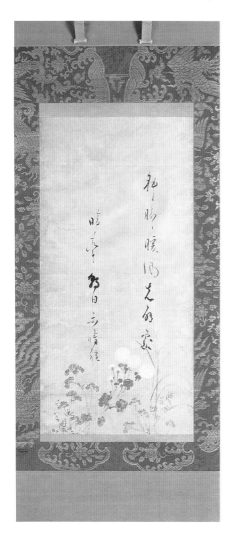

Hanging scrolls were mounted on to a silk brocade background into which wooden ends were inserted at top and bottom. They were rolled for storage or displayed in the *tokonoma*, an alcove found in traditional Japanese rooms. (No 18)

or scrolls: the hanging scroll 'Flower design for *Waka* poem' (No 18) is an example. The poems illustrate his communion with nature where he found universal themes of joy and sorrow which reflected the lives of the people surrounding him.

The traditions of Kōetsu and Sōtatsu were continued in the late seventeenth century in the work of Ogata Korin and his younger brother Ogata Kenzan. They also designed lacquer, and Kenzan made ceramics which sometimes used designs by his brother. Their father had been a Kyoto dyer associated with Kōetsu's colony of artists and craftsmen. The brothers moved to the new capital at Edo, hoping to find work and prosper. All Kenzan's paintings date from this period at the beginning of the eighteenth century and the style of his hanging scroll (No 22) is a development of the classical traditions revived by Kōetsu.

The use of the hanging scroll was related to another development in the interior architecture of a Japanese home. The *tokonoma* is an alcove found in Japanese rooms from the end of the fifteenth century. Its origins lie in the grouping, for devotional purposes, of icons in Zen chapels, after the rise of Zen Buddhism in the thirteenth century. The most important icon was the hanging scroll executed with a brush in ink on a white background. These scrolls were often executed by Zen monks in a state of enlightenment and could be in the form of a *koan*, riddle, used by their disciples as an aid to meditation. These *koans* were either quickly brushed pictures or poems with a hidden message which would lead the devotee to enlightenment.

Zen painting takes nature as its main subject. In Sesson's hands the brush indicates the strength in the wings of a dove (No 17). The filled sails of a boat sailing beneath the lofty heights of Mount Fuji in a painting by Shinsō illustrates the versatility of the brushstrokes (No 16). Both these paintings are from the sixteenth century. It was not until after the development of the tea ceremony in the fifteenth century that the use of the hanging scroll in the *tokonoma* became widespread.

The move to Edo by the Tokugawa shoguns at the beginning of the seventeenth century resulted in many social and economic changes. Three separate classes emerged, the samurai who were professional soldiers, farmers, and merchants. All owed allegiance to their feudal lord who served the shogun. The lords had to spend six months of the year in Edo, leaving their families there as hostages when visiting their territories. This created a stable system which gave peace to Japan for the next 270 years.

The growth of commerce and subsequent prosperity led to a samurai class in constant debt to the merchants as they tried to meet the needs of urban life. This exchange of wealth further stimulated the growth of trade. The rigid class structure left no opportunity for rising up the social scale, so energies were channelled into economic and cultural activities. The arts flourished, and later a popular culture emerged to suit more mercantile tastes. In this new centre of commerce the Edo artist developed new styles and forms for a thriving market. The wealthy patrons in Kyoto had preferred the hand-painted screen but in Edo the hanging scroll and wood-block print were thought to be lighter both in form and on the purse.

New styles were devoted to depicting scenes from everyday life, such as fair women and handsome men indulging in the pleasures of the entertainment quarter, actors playing their favourite roles in the theatre and views of famous places around the capital or of pilgrimage. Artists focused in close-up on the leading figures in this glamourous milieu, singly or in groups. These central themes of the popular prints of the next two hundred years distinguish *Ukiyoe* from any other school of Japanese art.

All the prints in the exhibition are from the nineteenth century. They are in two groups. The first comprises theatrical prints showing the famous actors of the day in their most popular roles (Nos 26–40). All the artists in this section worked in Osaka. The Osaka print artist almost always portrayed actors in current theatrical performances. Edo prints were readily available in Osaka, so the Osaka publishers, who had historical ties with the theatre, may have

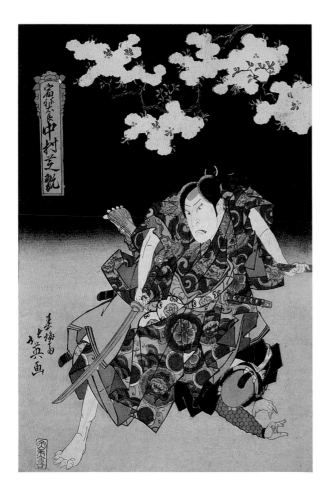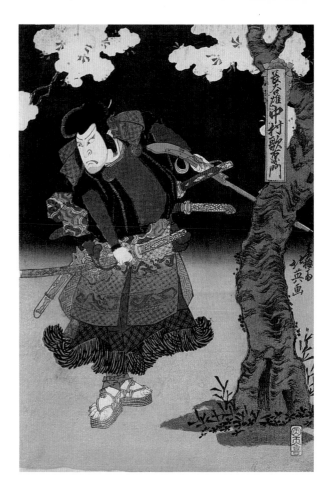

Two woodblock prints by Shunbaisai Hokuei showing the famous actors Nakamura Shikan II and Nakamura Utaemon III in favourite roles. (Nos 34, 35)

wished to monopolize a proven market rather than risk loss in competition with the popular products of the capital. It is important to remember that the print artist was a member of a team which produced the prints. While he was responsible for the design, it was carved out of the woodblock by the engraver, and the printer was responsible for transferring the final result to paper. The whole team was responsible to the publisher.

The second group is of landscape prints from three separate series. They are by Katsushika Hokusai (1760–1849) and

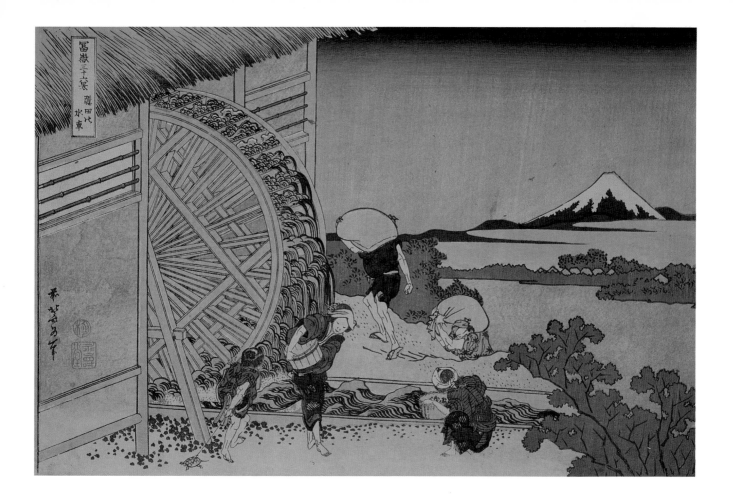

Utagawa Hiroshige (1797–1858), both prolific artists, but with different talents. Hiroshige was a master of the landscape print (Nos 36 and 37) and Hokusai excelled at peopling his landscapes with characters at work. Both artists did series of 'The fifty-three stations of the Tōkkaido road', recording their experiences of travelling along the main thoroughfare from Edo to Kyoto. Hiroshige's later versions are well known but it is the lesser known earlier series by Hokusai, concentrating on the travellers and the people he met, which is shown here (No 40).

It is still possible to see Mt Fuji from central Tokyo, but seldom as clearly as here in Hokusai's print of 'The Water Wheel at Onden', now an area of apartment blocks and unceasing traffic. (No 38)

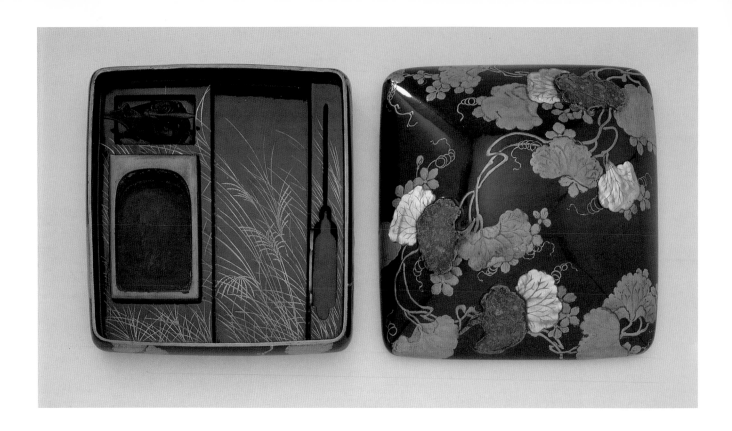

The decoration on this lacquer writing case is in the style of those designed by Hon'ami Kōetsu. (No 44)

The exhibition also shows what lies behind the screens in the form of lacquer furniture, beautifully crafted games and writing boxes. The Japanese often take as much care over the craftsmanship of their containers as they do the contents. Wrapping is an important cultural concept seen in many aspects of Japanese life. Boxes to hold a mask, *men*, or a sash, *obi*, were made with the particular object in mind. Picnic sets included a bottle and cups for sake and had a separate container for each course. All were beautifully decorated with a common theme which was often related to the season or occasion of the picnic.

The earliest lacquer pieces in the exhibition are the Negoro lacquers (Nos 74 and 75). This simple style using a red lacquer coating developed during the Muramachi period (1337–

1586), originated by the priests at the Negoro Temple, although no surviving pieces can be traced back to the temple. With use, the black undercoat shows through, giving the pieces added beauty still very much appreciated and copied in Japan today.

Small lacquer containers, *inrō*, were worn hung from the *obi* at the waist. This habit was adopted generally at the end of the sixteenth century. At first they were used to carry the ink for personal seals. Their tightly-fitted layered compartments were later found indispensable for the carrying of drugs and herbs, after patent medicines became widely available in the latter half of the seventeenth century (Nos 62–70).

The last group of objects in the exhibition belonged to the samurai, the warriors of medieval Japan who served their masters, the *daimyo*. Armour was not only worn in battle but also when, on ceremonial occasions, audiences were given. It was made of light, lacquered metal or leather plates fastened with silk laces. Various styles developed with innovations following changes in the needs of the battlefield.

Ōyoroi was the loose-fitting defensive armour of the mounted archers developed late in the Heian period (794–1185). *Dōmaru* armour has a continuous sheath-like cuirass which is thought to have been developed as the armour of the common foot-soldier in the Heian period. By the Edo period both were worn only on ceremonial occasions (Nos 87 and 91).

 Gusaku armour was first produced in the sixteenth century. To allow more movement, the cuirass was divided into two or five sections made of laminated tiers or long horizontal plates (Nos 88–90). Helmets for this type of armour were often idiosyncratic in style and there are examples of these in the exhibition (Nos 93 and 94).

Swords were the most important weapon of the samurai, who were allowed to wear two, a long one and a short one. Important blades were given individual names, and the history of their performance in battle was well known. The earliest blade in

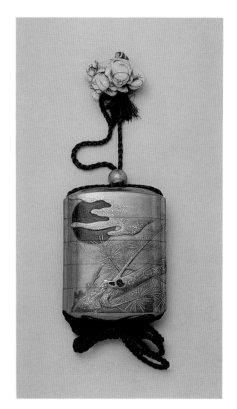

Inrō, small personal containers, were beautifully decorated, as illustrated in this view of the other side of that shown on page 83. (No 69)

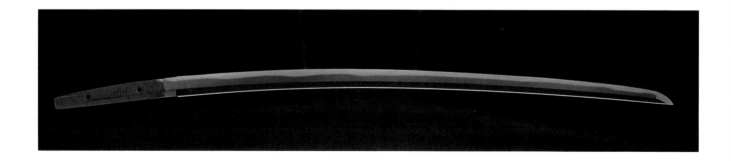

This sword blade made in the 11th century is the earliest object in the exhibition. (No 108)

The 12th-century battle of Ichinotani, illustrated on the screen from which this detail is taken, shows examples of contemporary arms and armour. (No 11)

the exhibition dates from 1027–37, in the Heian period. The curved blade is typical of the Japanese sword developed at this time.

Swordsmiths ranked highly in their class and even emperors were known to forge blades. Blades were made from layers of tempered steel, welded and then folded back upon themselves. The process was repeated until there were many thousands of layers of steel. Throughout the process there were prescribed Shinto rituals ensuring the purity of the blade's manufacture. The last and most important stage, before handing over to the sharpener was to temper the edge by alternately dipping it in fire and water. This allowed the edge to take on the sharpness of a razor while the blade remained flexible and would not snap with hard usage. Swords are often admired for the straight or irregular patterns which define this hard tempered edge.

Blades were often mounted into wooden hilts covered with the white noduled skin of the rayfish and bound with silk cord, using a set of beautifully decorated sword furniture (No 109). After the unification of Japan in the seventeenth century under the Tokugawa shoguns, these mounts became more decorative. Traditionally made of iron, softer metals such as silver, bronze and copper were used alongside three special copper alloys peculiar to Japan. From 1600 bold sculpture was used along with the earlier methods of engraving and coarse inlay, leading to a highly decorative style.

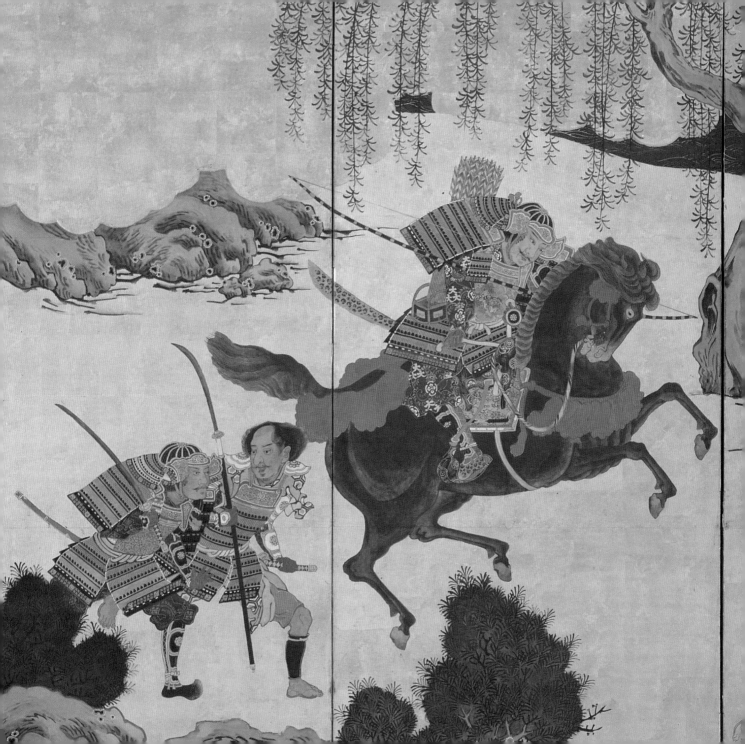

During the Edo period fear of invasion by western powers resulted in a policy of isolation. Japan closed her ports to all foreign trade with the exception of the Dutch and the Chinese who were restricted to trading through Nagasaki in the far south. Foreign influence on goods made for the domestic market lessened and a purely Japanese style evolved.

In 1868 the Meiji Emperor set up his Imperial palace in Tokyo. His restoration was achieved partly because of the failure of the Tokugawa shogunate to maintain the isolation of Japan. Popular sentiment ran high against the opening of the country to trade with the West and the unequal treaties that were forced on Japan. Competition remained throughout this period between adherents of Japanese traditions and those promoting western trends.

The two succeeding Emperors, Taishō (1912–26), and Shōwa (1926–89), saw the rapid modernization of Japan and its consequences. With the succession passing to Emperor Akihito on the death of his father in 1989 Japan moved into a new phase of history. Although the claim to divinity was given up after the Second World War, the Emperor is still a revered figurehead in Japan. His role is similar to that of the British Monarch. He is consulted and advised, but has no actual power in the democratic government of the country.

Today Japanese businessmen, designers and technicians set world trends. Their success is rooted as much in the traditional values of their unique culture as in their ability to assimilate new ideas.

SCREENS

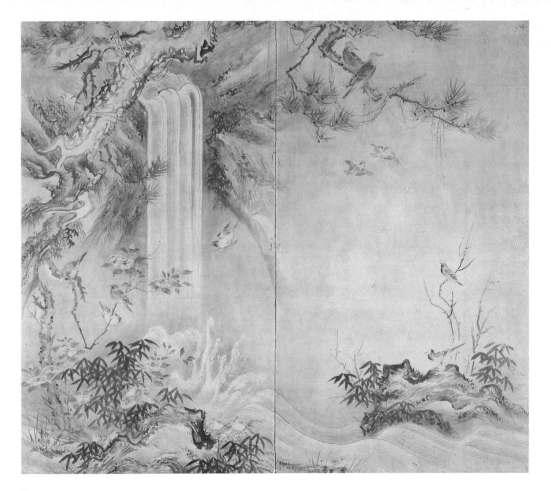

1

Waterfall and little birds

Folding screen
Kanō Eitoku
Momoyama Period
161.1 × 186.0 cm

Birds and a waterfall far up the mountain are painted in the fine light and shade of *sumi* ink. Gold paste, lightly covering the blank space, adds colour to the screen. The waterfall is the main feature with pine trees, a pool, bamboo trees and rocks. This is a masterpiece of the Momoyama period, with a typical dynamism expressed by the spraying waterfall contrasting with flitting birds.

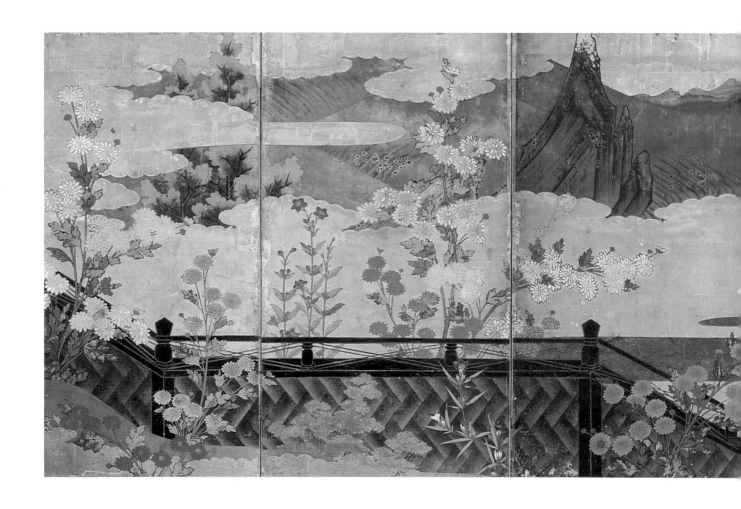

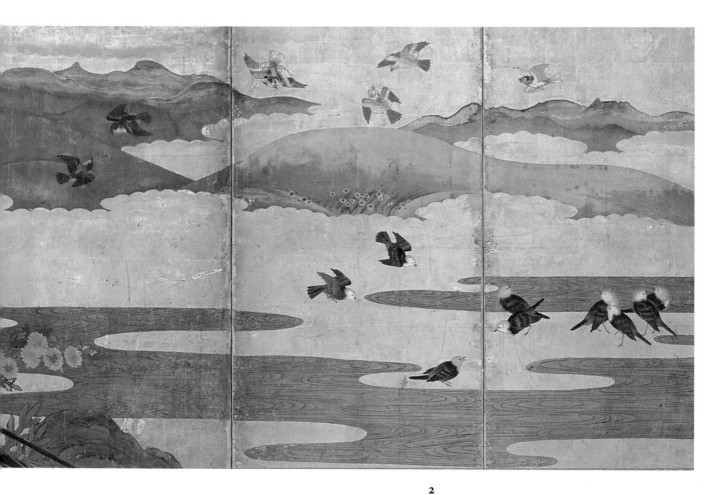

2

Birds and flowers

Folding screen

Tosa School
Momoyama Period
94.8×287.8 cm

Six-fold screen, colours over gold leaf on paper .

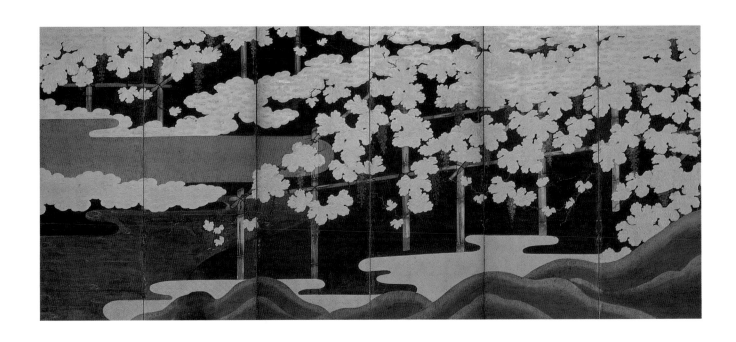

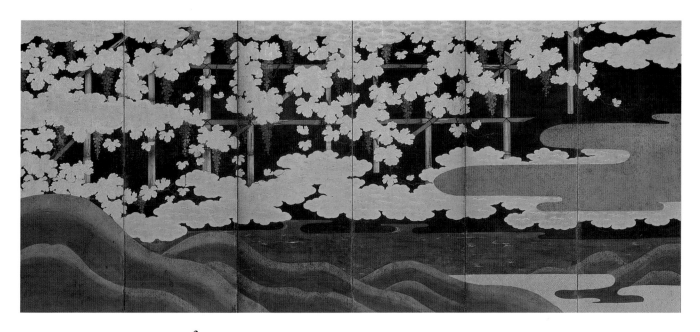

3

Grape arbour

Pair of folding screens (details illustrated on front and back covers)

Kanō School
Momoyama Period
166.3 × 287.8 cm

Grape vines cover an arbour, creating a rich autumnal atmosphere. Vine leaves and gold clouds are decoratively represented by piling up *gofun* powder (white chalk) – a technique also found in lacquer-work. The bank and running water in the lower part of the screen give it depth. From the late Momoyama to the early Edo period, artists often adopted a single motif for screen painting. This is attributed to the late Momoyama period.

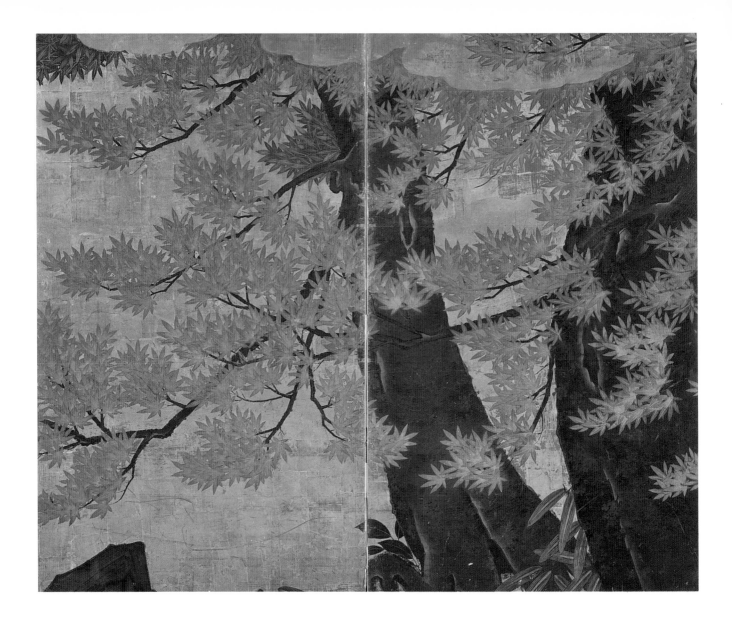

4

Maple leaves

Folding screen

Artist unknown
Momoyama Period
145.8 × 176.8 cm

A maple tree in autumn is painted on a gold,
two-fold screen. It is full of the dynamic spirit
characteristic of the Momoyama period.
Sasanqua flowers and evergreen leaves, which
are probably of the *madake* (a common
Japanese bamboo), are depicted at the base of
the maple. The crimson leaves are a symbol of
autumn, while cherry blossom represents
spring, and their use in paintings and poetry is
an ancient tradition. They are often the subject
of *waka* (31-syllable poems).

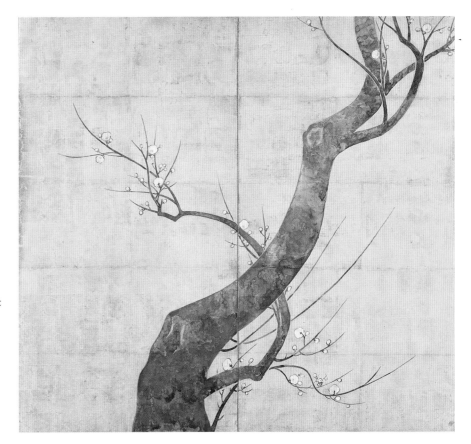

5

Plum tree

Folding screen

Rimpa School
Edo Period
169.2 × 182.0 cm

Two-fold screen, colours over gold leaf on
paper

6

Pine trees and cherry blossoms

Folding screen

Attributed to Tawaraya Sōtatsu (died about
1640)
Early Edo Period
155.0×355.0 cm

A group of pine trees diagonally divide the
screen from upper right to lower left. The bold
composition and the technique employed in
painting the pines and the trunks of the cherry
trees are characteristic of Sōtatsu. It is reminiscent of his painting of *The Pine Tree* at *Yogen-in*,
a temple in Kyoto, with its contrasting green
surface and gold foundation, and of his
Tsutano Hosomichi folding screens, which have
calligraphy by Karasumaru Mitsuhiro.
Although the link is not close, the delicate
style is similar. This painting has no signature
or seal, but if the artist is Sōtatsu, it could
belong to the transition period which shows
his abstract use of colour, as seen in the *Tsutano
Hosomichi* screen. The cherry blossoms in full
bloom painted in the upper right are the result
of thickly heaped colour, and the pine needles
are depicted with complete success. The
overall effect is remarkably organic to the
screen.

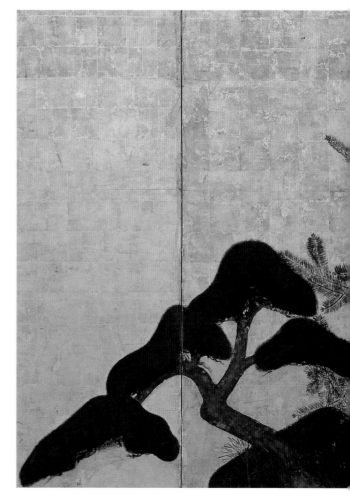

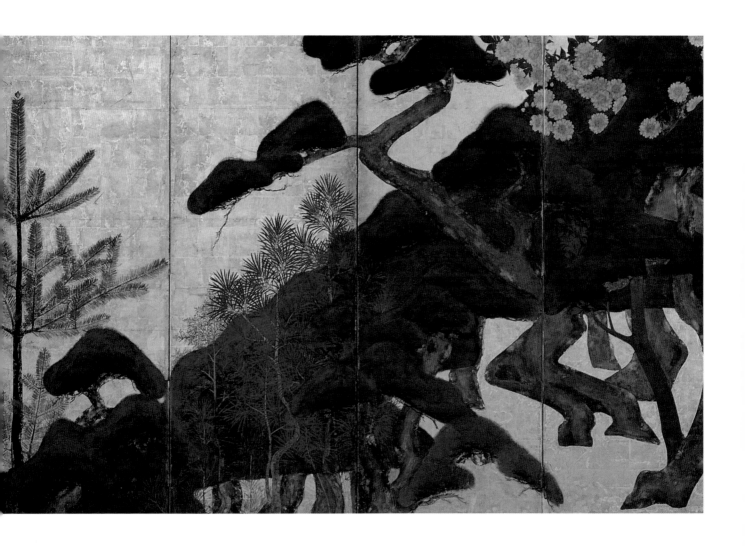

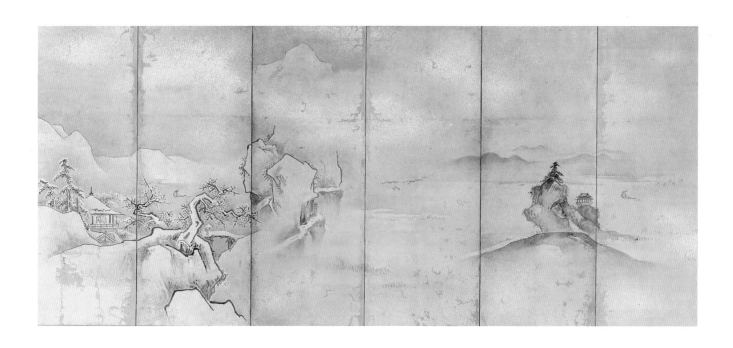

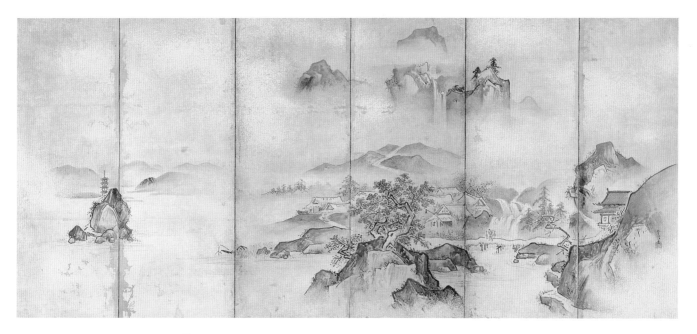

7

The four seasons

Pair of folding screens (detail illustrated on
page 5)

Kanō Tsunenobu (1636–1713)
Early Edo Period
174.0×375.2 cm

The seasonal changes of the landscape are
presented from the right side panel to the left.
The painter, Kanō Tsunenobu was a talented
leader of the Edo Kanō school. Due to his
successful career, the Kanōs were granted a
hereditary position as painters-in-ordinary to
the shogunate.

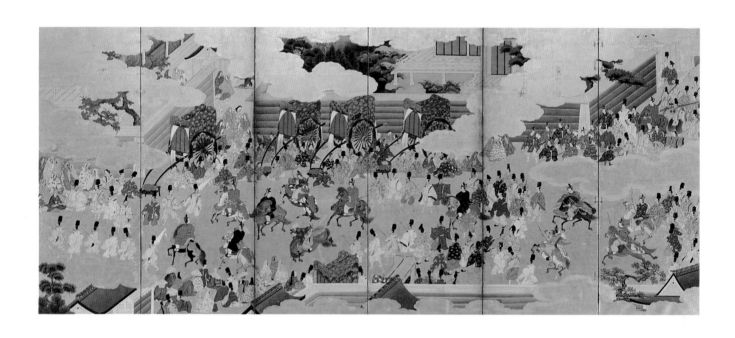

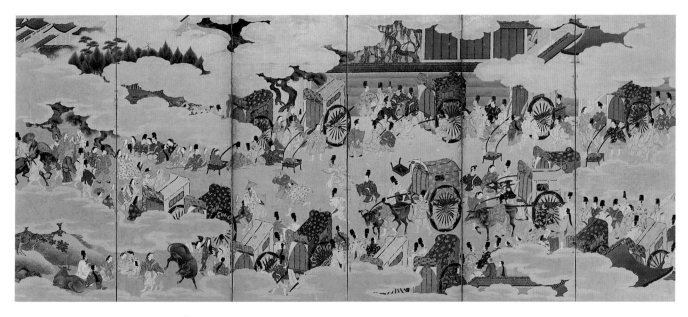

8

Scenes from the *Tale of Genji*

Pair of folding screens (detail illustrated on page x)

Tosa School
Edo Period
122.1 × 288.0 cm

The panels show several scenes from the *Tale of Genji*, The episodes illustrated are not linked, but each closely follows the story. The work with its fine detail using the technique typical of the Tosa school in *yamato-e* is of the highest quality.

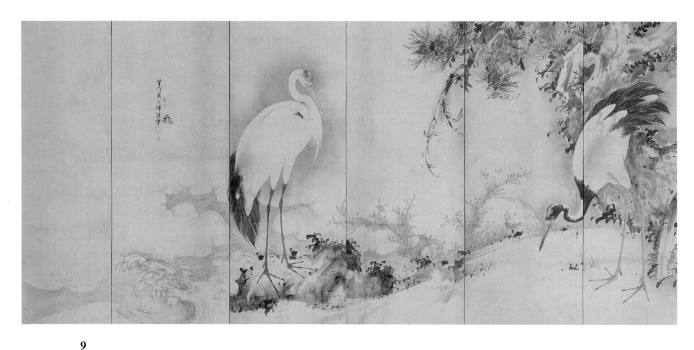

9

Cranes

Folding screen

Sōga Shōhaku (1730–81)
Mid-Edo Period
173.8 × 396.2 cm

This is the left panel of a pair of screens painted with *sumi* ink by Sōga Shōhaku. In spite of the moral restrictions of the Edo period he led an easy life. Two cranes are graciously painted, with a pine tree, waves and rocks in the background. Its graduated tone gives a depth to the screen.

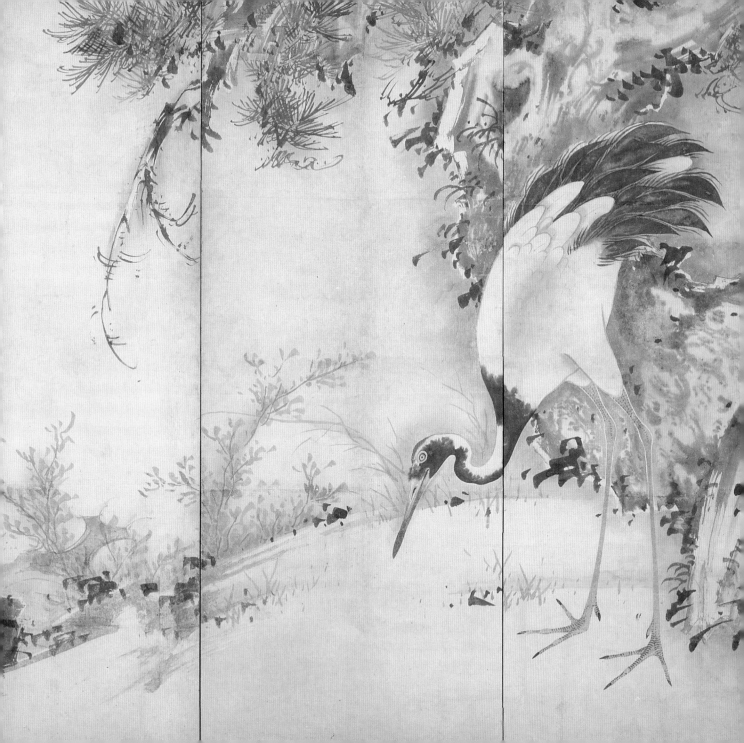

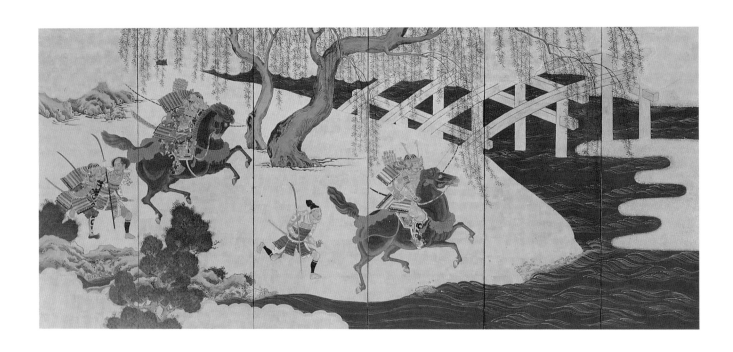

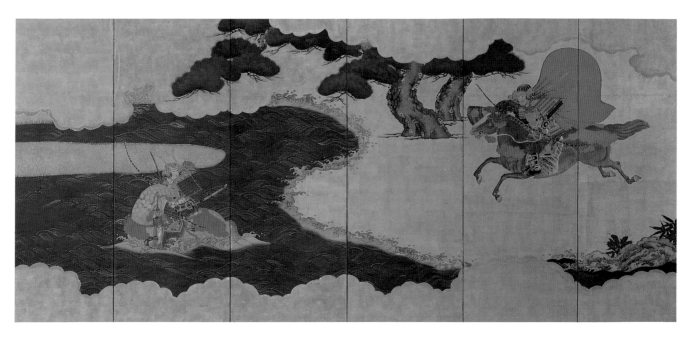

10, 11

The battle scenes at Ichinotani and the Uji River

Folding screen (detail illustrated on page 19)

Tosa School
Edo Period
172.8 × 371.2cm

These gold screen panels show the famous episodes at Ichinotani (11) and the Uji river (10) from the Gempei battle in the *Heike Monogatari* (the historic romance of the Taira family). Among the paintings of ancient warriors from the Muromachi period onward, these two battle scenes occur most frequently. The striking red provides a beautiful contrast to the blue green of pine and willow trees, and to the deep blue of the waters. The drawing of the figures is elaborate. On the Ichinotani panel are depicted the contrasting characters of Kumagaya Naozane, a fierce warrior, and Taira no Atsumori, an aristocrat. On the Uji river panel, Sasaki Takatsuna and Kajiwara no Kagesue are competing to lead the van.

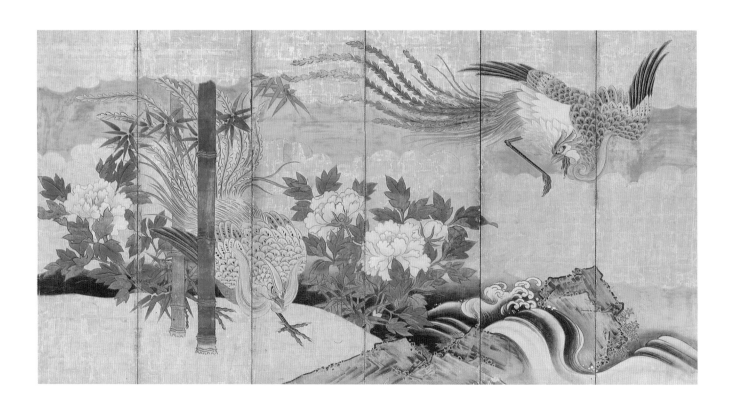

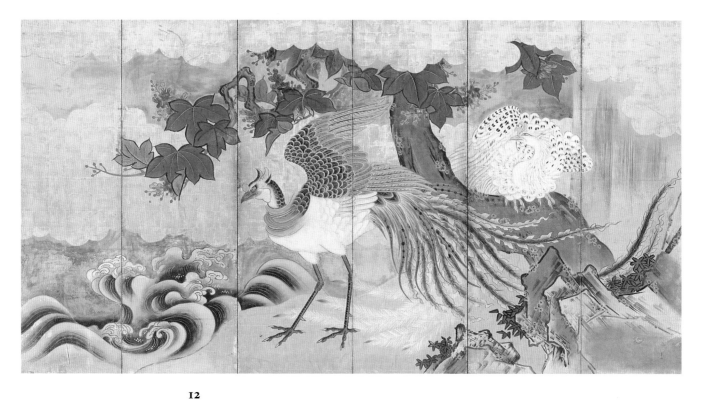

12

Chinese phoenix

Pair of folding screens (detail illustrated on page 9)

Kanō School
Edo Period
203.0×774.8 cm

The phoenix is an imaginary bird esteemed in ancient China. It is believed that it combines the characteristics of different animals. It is believed to have feathers of five colours, to roost in the blue paulownia, feeding on bamboo nuts, and to have eternal life. It is a traditional motif in Chinese painting, which was introduced to Japan and portrayed in a Japanese style. The phoenix was an auspicious symbol. Here a pair of male and female phoenixes are depicted with bamboo trees and peony flowers on the left, and with paulownia trees on the right. The thick and heavy lines, particular to the Kanō school, create a virile effect.

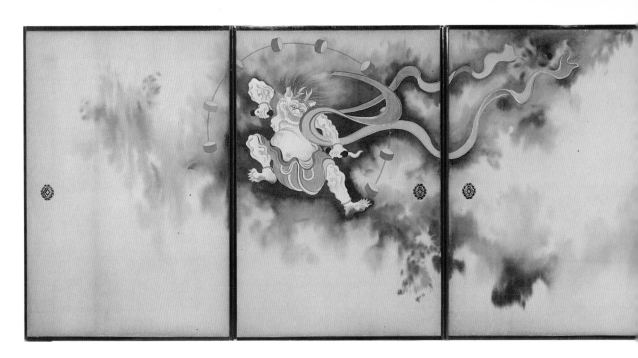

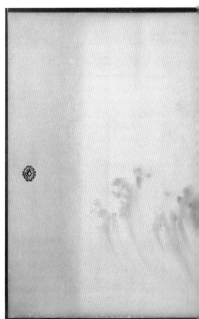

13

Fujin and Raijin, the gods of wind and thunder

Sliding screens (double-sided, detail illustrated on page 3)

Suzuki Kiitsu (1796–1858)
Late Edo Period
173.8 × 484.0

The gods Fujin and Raijin are a major motif adopted by the masters of the Rimpa school: Tawaraya Sōtatsu, Ogata Korin, Sakai Hōitsu and others. This screen is by Suzuki Kiitsu, a student of Hōitsu. Each side of the panel shows one of the gods. The clouds, painted in the *tarashikomi* (spreading paste) technique, add variety and movement. The dynamic touch of the brush effectively expresses the broad sky, harmonizing beautifully with the gods of wind and thunder.

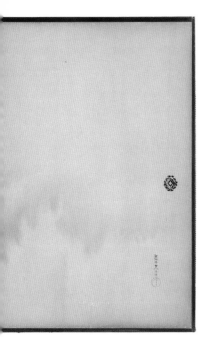

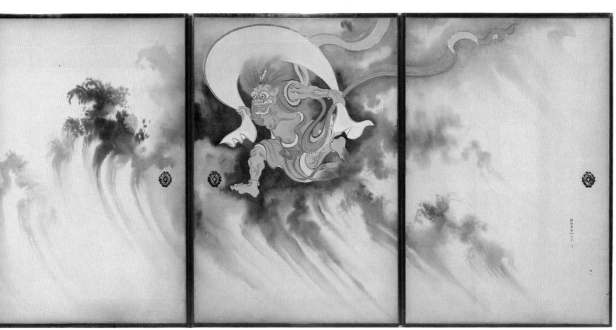

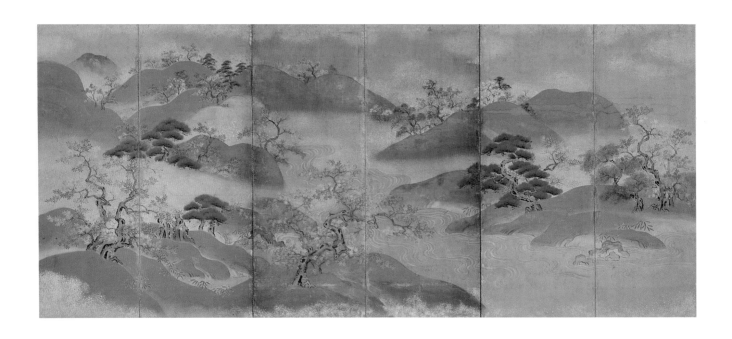

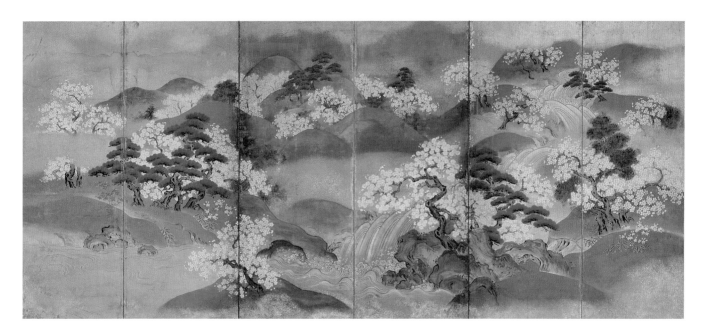

14

Mt Yoshino and the Tatsuta river

Pair of folding screens (details illustrated on pages ii and 121)

Kanō School
Edo Period
160.5 × 367.0 cm

Mt Yoshino and the Tatsuta river are places in the Nara prefecture celebrated for their beautiful cherry blossoms and maple leaves. These appear as motifs of spring and autumn in the *waka* (31-syllable Japanese poem), and also in traditional *Yamato-e* painting. With the clouds painted in gold leaf and powders and the delicate lines of the stream, seasonal contrast is vividly expressed by cherry blossoms and tinted autumnal leaves.

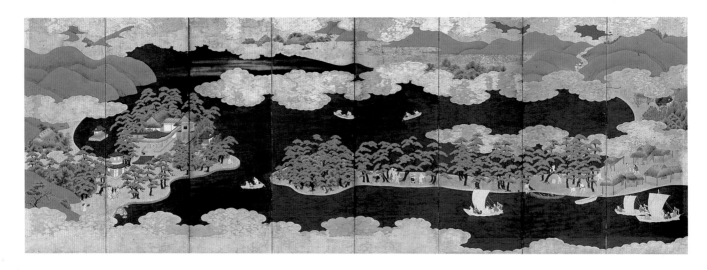

15

Scenes from *Ama-no-Hashidate*

Folding screen (detail illustrated on page vi)

Artist unknown
Edo Period
175.2 × 496.0 cm

Eight-fold screen, colours over gold leaf on
paper

PAINTINGS AND PRINTS

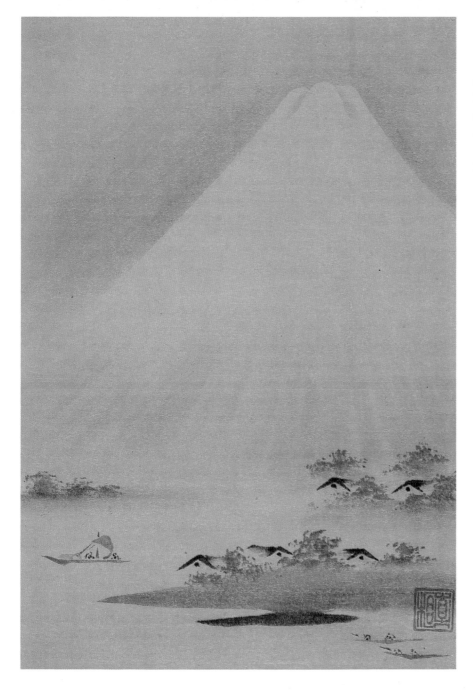

16

Mt Fuji

Hanging scroll

Shinsō (died 1525)
Muromachi Period
105.0×46.5 cm

Ink and colour on paper

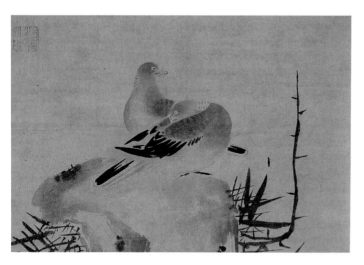

17
Doves
Hanging scroll
Sesson Shukei
Muromachi Period
31.0×45.3 cm

Ink and colour on paper

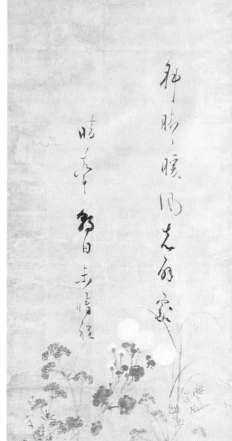

18

Illustrated *waka* poem with autumnal flowers

Hanging scroll
Hon'ami Kōetsu (1558–1637)
Momoyama Period
83.0×43.0 cm

The following verse is written in soft brush strokes on a space illustrated with autumnal chrysanthemums and *ominaeshi* in gold leaf:

There's a drizzle of spring rains falling
Here's a mild eastern wind blowing askingly
The rain sounds softly in the dark
The shade of the morning still remains

19, 20

Journey to the east/Yearning for a loved one

Pair of scrolls

Kanō Toun Masunobu (1625–94)
Edo Period
123.0 × 51.3 cm

Azuma Kudari (Journey to the east) is an
episode in the *Ise Story*. It is the travel journal
of a hero, Ariwara-no-Narihira, said to be also
a poet. This episode has a long tradition as a
theme in paintings. One of the pair of screens,
Sofu Koi (Yearning for a loved one), represents
a famous short story in which Minamoto-no
Nakakuni, ordered by the Emperor, traced
Kogō no Tsubone, who isolated herself from
society and lived in Saga, Kyoto, through the
tune she is playing. This pair of scrolls contrast
spring and autumn. The feelings of the man
and woman are expressed through the simple
brushwork characteristic of the Kanō school in
Edo.

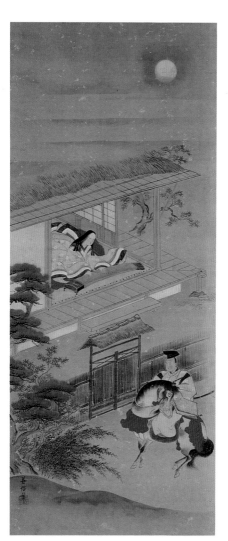
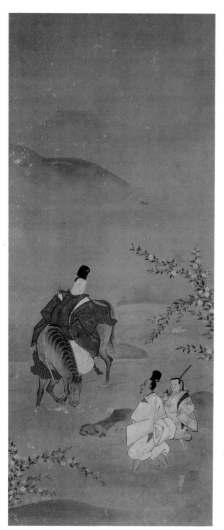

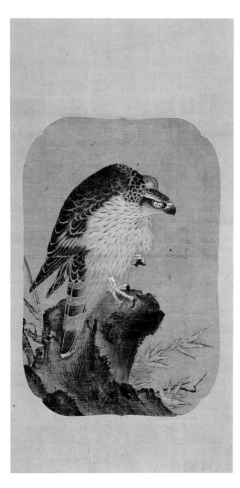

Wild cherry blossoms

Hanging scroll

Ogata Kenzan (1663–1743)
Early Edo Period
99.0 × 24.5 cm

In the rectangular space, hillocks, represented by spreading gold paste, are set with cherry flowers shaped like *bonsai* (dwarf trees). Although the gold trunks and silver petals of the cherry flowers are highly decorative, the entire impression remains warm and soft. It is well known that Kenzan was a younger brother of Ogata Korin, and a potter of Kyoto ware. All of his paintings are attributed to the Kyōhō period (early 18th century) when he moved to Edo. His seal, *Kenzan*, also uses gold paste.

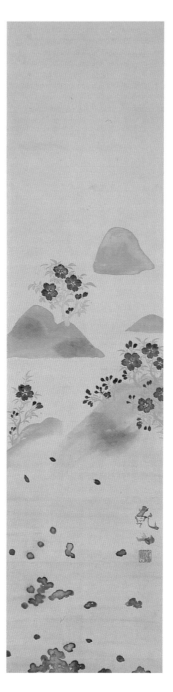

21

Hawk

Hanging scroll

Kanō School
Edo Period
51.0 × 35.5 cm

Ink and colour on paper

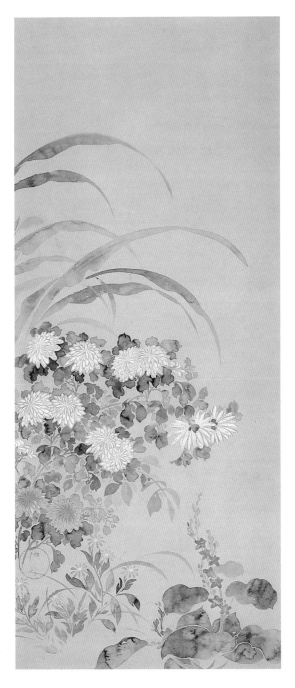

23
Chrysanthemums

Hanging scroll
Rimpa School
Edo Period
125.0 × 53.5 cm

Colour on silk

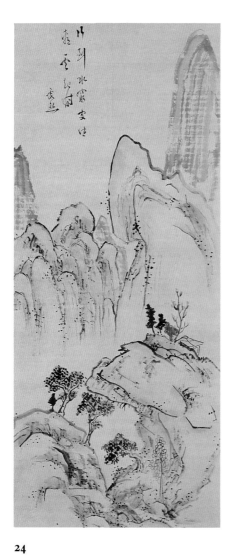

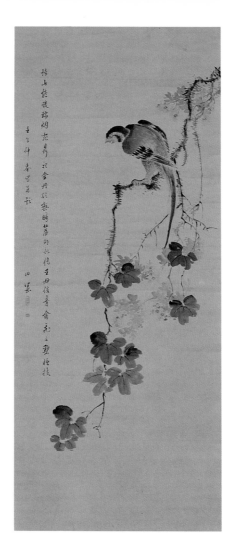

24

Landscape

Hanging scroll

Ikeno Taiga (1723–76)

Mid-Edo Period

131.2 × 55.5 cm

Colour on paper

25

Birds and flowers

Hanging scroll

Tanomura Chikuden (1777–1835)

Late Edo Period

119.0 × 51.0 cm

Colour on paper

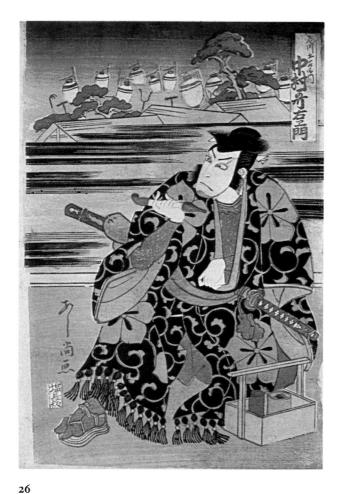

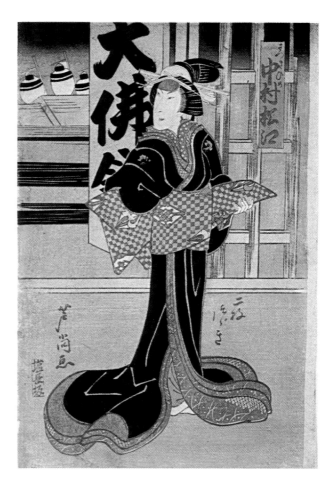

26

Nakamura Utaemon Ⅲ in the role of
Ishikawa Goemon

Colour print

Ashitaka
1817, Late Edo Period
38.5 × 26.5 cm

27

Nakamura Matsue Ⅲ in the role of
Satsuki

Colour print

Ashitaka
1817, Late Edo Period
39.0 × 26.5 cm

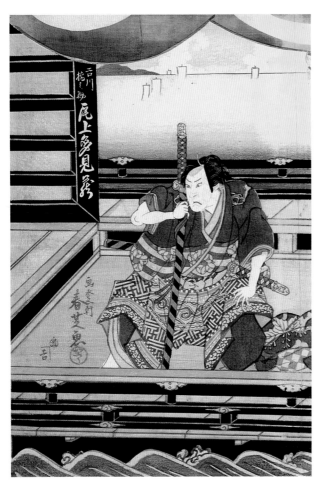

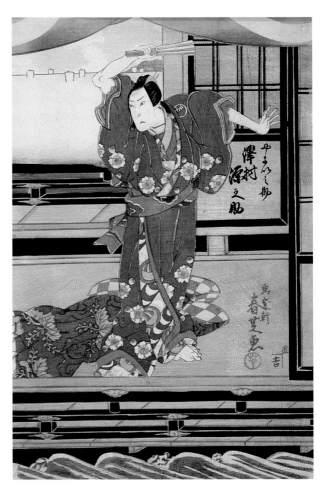

28

Onoe Tamizō II in the role of
Yoshikawa Hashinosuke

Colour print

Gatōken Shunshi
1826, Late Edo Period
40.0 × 27.6 cm

29

**Sawamura Gennosuke II in the role
of** *Yayoinosuke*

Colour print

Gatoken Shunshi
1826, Late Edo Period
39.0 × 27.0 cm

30

Arashi Tomasiburō in the role of
Arimaya Ofuji **and Nakamura Karoku**
in the role of *Nodaya Ofuji*

Colour print

Gigadō Ashiyuki
1825, Late Edo Period
39.0 × 27.0 cm

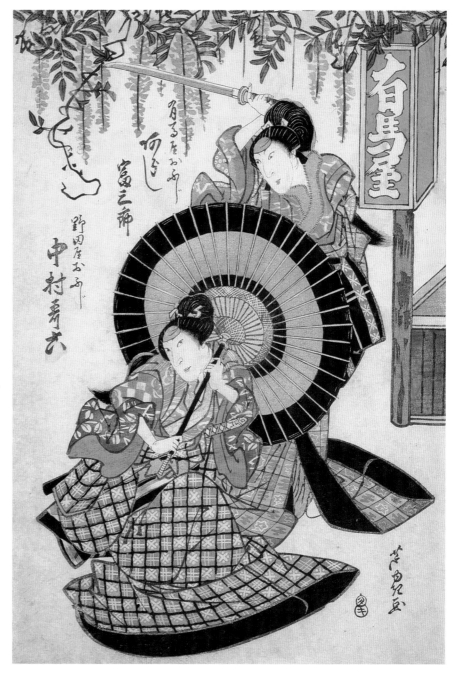

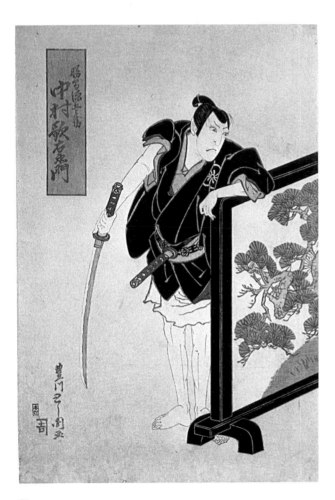

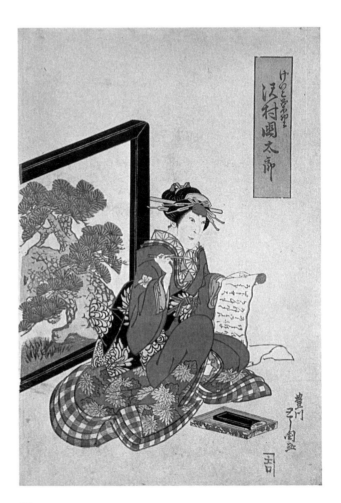

31

Nakamura Utaemon in the role of
Katsuma Gengobei

Colour print

Juyōdō Toshikuni
1826, Late Edo Period
38.0 × 26.5 cm

32

Sawamura Kunitarō in the role of the
Geisha *Kikuno*

Colour print

Juyōdō Toshikuni
1826, Late Edo Period
39.5 × 27.5 cm

33

Nakamura Matsue in the role of the courtesan *Namiji*

Colour print

Ryūsai Shigeharu (1803–53)
1831, Late Edo Period
38.5 × 26.5 cm

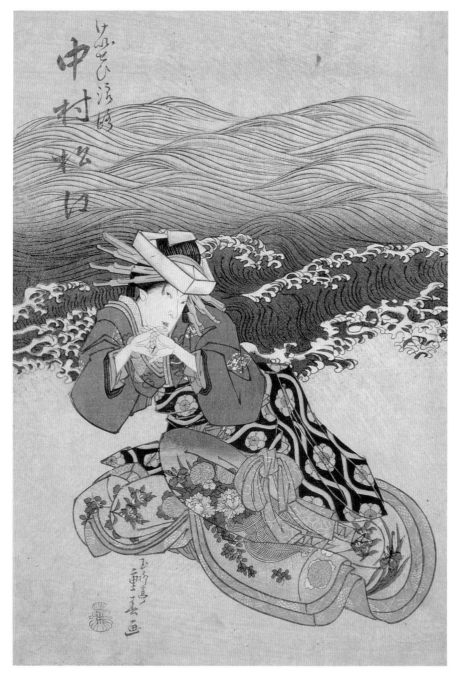

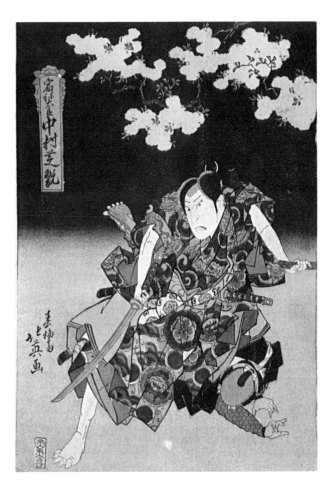

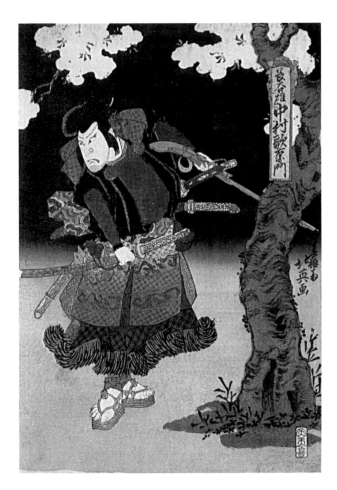

34

Nakamura Shikan II in the role of
Shikune no Taro

Colour print

Shunbaisai Hokuei (died 1837)
1834, Late Edo Period
38.5 × 27.0 cm

35

Nakamura Utaemon III in the role of
Kino Haseo

Colour print

Shunbaisai Hokuei (died 1837)
1834, Late Edo Period
38.5 × 27.0 cm

36

A hundred celebrated places in Edo

Shower over the Ō-hashi Bridge, Atake

Colour print

Utagawa Hiroshige (1797–1858)
1858, Late Edo Period
35.7 × 24.7 cm

Atake, dimly seen to the right over the
Ō-hashi bridge, is the name of a place. This
evening scene shows a sudden shower, with
people trotting along with umbrellas or a straw
raincoat. The distant shore is in heavy rain.
This is one of a series of several prints. In
another version, there are ferry boats along the
riverside and gathering low-hanging rain
clouds. The version here is considered to be
the first edition.

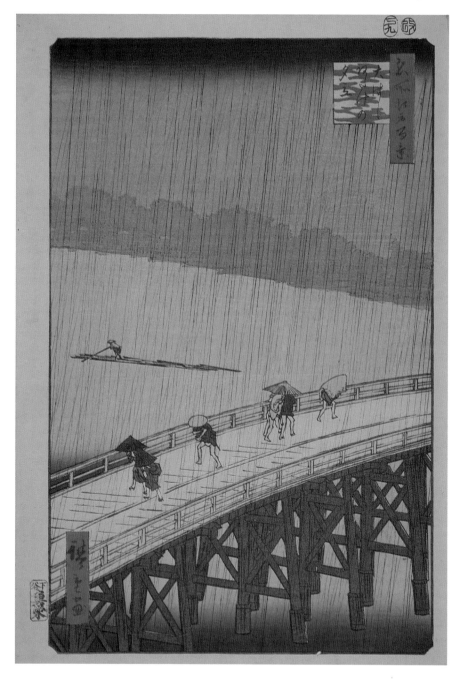

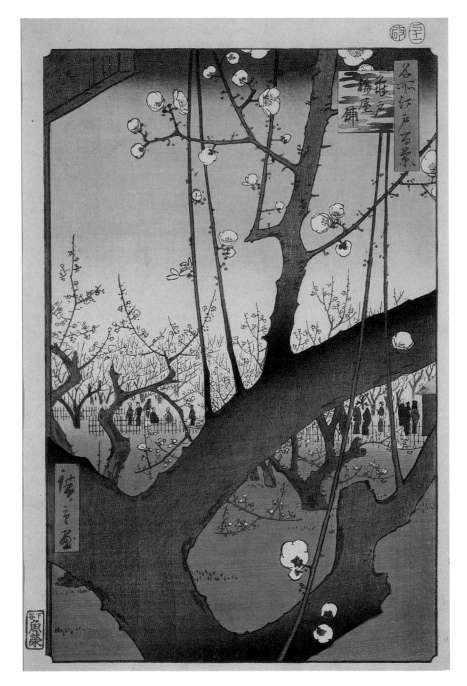

37

A hundred celebrated places in Edo

Plum garden at Kameido

Colour print

Utagawa Hiroshige (1797–1858)
1858, Late Edo Period
36.8 × 25.0 cm

The series entitled *A hundred places of scenic
beauty Edo* was produced between 1856 and
1858, and the 118 pieces of the series are the
masterpieces of Hiroshige's latter years. With
the excellent technique of the engraver and
printer, this series is a landmark in the modernization of Japanese painting, and also rounds off
Hiroshige's career. The old *Garyubai* (reclining
dragon-like plum tree) at the Kameido plum
garden was appreciated as 'the best plum tree in
Edo', and attracted many visitors. Hiroshige
puts one particular tree in the foreground. It is
well known that Van Gogh, the Dutch late
impressionist, copied both this work and
'Shower over the Ōhashi Bridge, Atake'.

38

Thirty-six views of Mt Fuji

Waterwheel at Onden

Colour print (illustrated on page 15)

Katsushika Hokusai (1760–1849)
Late Edo Period
26.0 × 38.5 cm

Onden is located between Harajuku and
Aoyama in Tokyo. In the late Edo period it
was a quiet rural area, and the waterwheel
beside the Shibuya river was a well-known
famous spot. Beyond the waterwheel is Mt
Fuji in the mist, with in the foreground men
carrying sacks of grain and women preparing
rice. The scene is typical of Hokusai's great
interest in daily life and its characters.

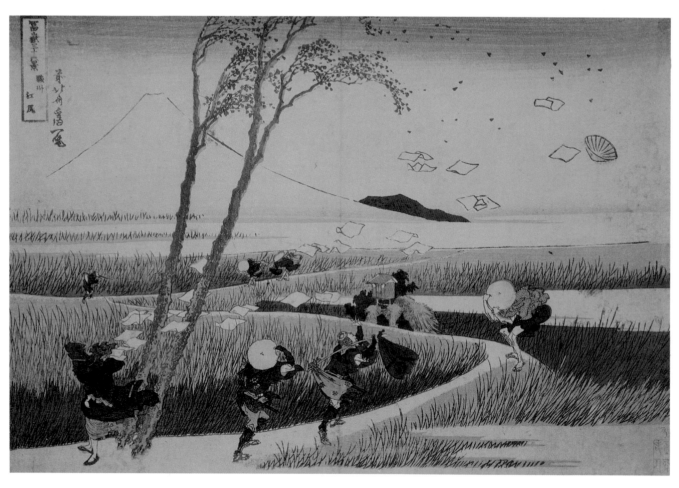

39

Thirty-six views of Mt Fuji

Ejiri in Suruga Province

Colour print

Katsushika Hokusai (1760–1849)
Late Edo Period
24.2 × 36.2 cm

Ejiri used to be the post town along the Tōkaidō next to Shimizu harbour, in Shimizu city, Shizuoka prefecture. The strong wind is bending the trees and blowing a straw hat and papers up in the air, providing a distinctive contrast to the calmness of Mt Fuji in the background.

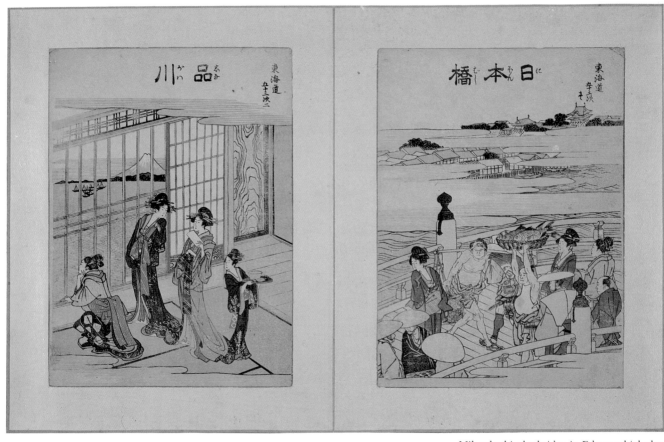

Nihonbashi, the bridge in Edo at which the Tōkkaidō began, and Shinagawa, the first station.

40

Fifty-three stations of the Tōkaidō

Colour print

Katsushika Hokusai (1760–1849)
1827, Late Edo Period
23.3 × 17.3 cm

The series *Fifty-three stations of the Tōkaidō* illustrates the post towns between Edo and Kyoto. The oldest *ukiyo-e* (Japanese genre painting) was painted by Hishikawa Moronobu. However, Hokusai was the first to paint a picture of a post station. This is one of his four series depicting the Tōkaidō stations. While the series by Utagawa Hiroshige is orthodox landscape prints, Hokusai's is better described as genre painting, on account of the impressiveness of the figures.

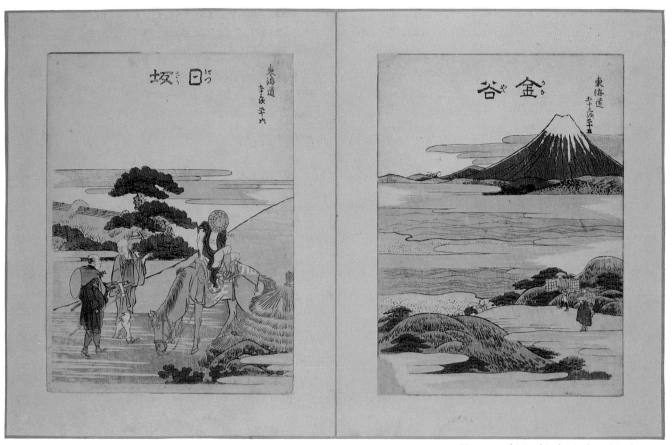

Kanaya and Nissaki, the 24th and 25th
stations on the Tōkkaidō.

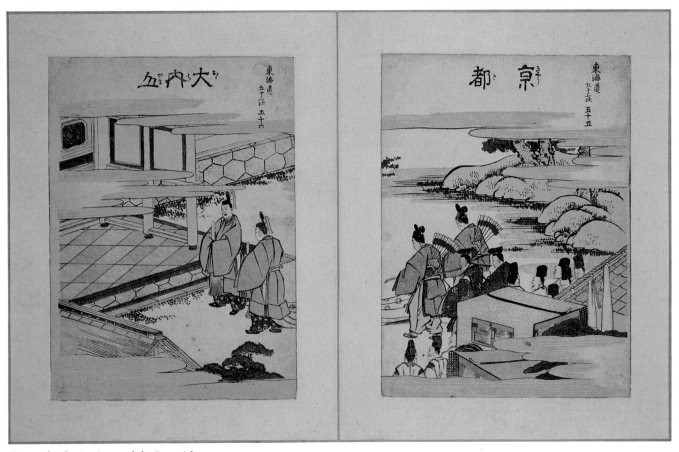

Kyoto, the destination, and the Imperial
Palace, Ōuchiyama in Kyoto.

LACQUER

41

Writing case in *maki-e* lacquer

Design of willow, bridge and watermill

Mid-Edo Period

24.5 × 22.1 × 5.1 cm

A writing case is a traditional stationery set produced from the late Heian period. As furnishings in the Court were formalized, the writing set, including an inkstone, brushes, a little pitcher and knife, became one of the indoor accessories. It remained until recently an important item of stationery. The surface of this lid is finished with n*ashiji* lacquer, and willow, bridge, watermill and working fishermen are depicted in *taka* (high relief) *maki-e* lacquer with an inlay of lead plate. This composition, which depicts the view at the Uji bridge in Kyoto, is called *Yanagi Hashi Suisha Zu* (willow, bridge, watermill). It has been a favourite subject of paintings since the Momoyama period. With the autumnal chrysanthemum and pampas grass, it is characteristically Japanese in style.

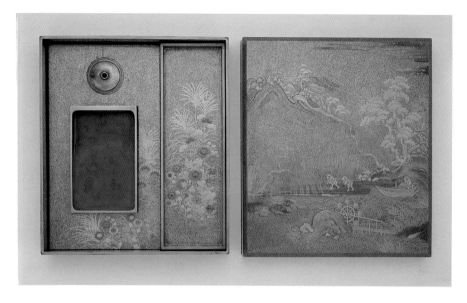

42

Writing case in *maki-e* lacquer

Design of peony

Mid- to Late Edo Period

23.7 × 21.9 × 4.6 cm

Two blooming peonies are painted on the surface of the lid, in *taka* (high relief) *maki-e* lacquer with gold leaf. The plants spread across the space. The large size of the flowers compared with the stems creates a florid effect. The contrast between the dark pear-skin lacquered base and the gold peony flowers in *taka maki-e* is strikingly beautiful. An inkstone, a little pitcher, writing brushes and a little knife, make up the set.

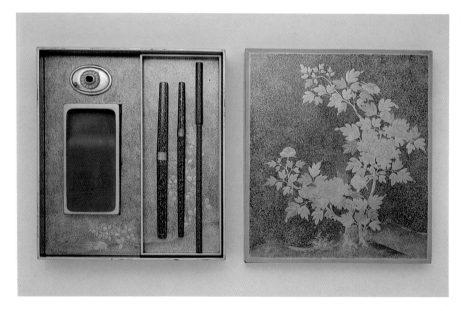

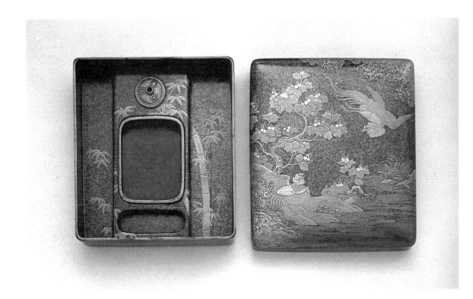

43

Writing case in *maki-e* lacquer

Design of paulownia and Chinese phoenix

Mid-Edo Period

22.8 × 20.6 × 4.6 cm

The surface of the lid is decorated in *taka* (high relief) *maki-e* lacquer with two Chinese phoenix birds and paulownia trees at the waterside. A Chinese phoenix is an imaginary bird of luck, traditionally esteemed in China. It was believed that its feathers were of five colours and that it roosted in the blue paulownia, picking up bamboo nuts. It was a traditional subject in Chinese painting, and was introduced to Japan at an early stage. It took root as a symbol in Japanese culture. The bamboo trees are lacquered in *taka maki-e*. The rich and complex decoration reflects a trend in the mid-Edo period.

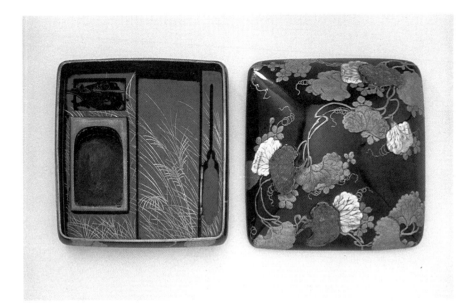

44

Writing case with inlay in *maki-e* lacquer

Design of bottle gourd

Mid- to Late Edo Period

22.8 × 22.5 × 10.1 cm

The lid is rounded at the corners and extended into a unique shape, like the famous writing case worked by Hon'ami Kōetsu. The design of bottle gourds is painted in *taka* (high relief) *maki-e* lacquer, with inlay work of mother-of-pearl and lead plate. A bottle gourd, featured in the volume 'Bottle Gourd' of the *Tale of Genji*, is a symbol of chastity and frailty made use of in artistic design. The characteristics of these Kōetsu *maki-e* are the selection of subjects from the classics, original design, usage of new materials such as lead and tin and the generous and decorative style.

45, 46
Writing case and table in *maki-e*
Design of the view of Uji

Late Edo Period
25.3 × 22.2 × 5.0 cm
61.1 × 34.8 × 11.8 cm

Bundai is a writing table with a paper weight at either end. Writing tables are often in a set with a writing case to match. Generally, the writing case and table together symbolize the world of poetry. In the Muromachi period, they were a feature of interior decoration. This writing case is decorated with a view of Uji in Kyoto, the writing table with the scenery around the Uji bridge. Around the gold-leaf bridge are pine trees, clouds and mist veiling the distant mountains in *taka* (high relief) *maki-e*. A flight of herons over the river is inlaid in silver. On the surface of the lid, is the Phoenix hall of the Byōdō-in temple depicted behind pine trees in *taka maki-e*.

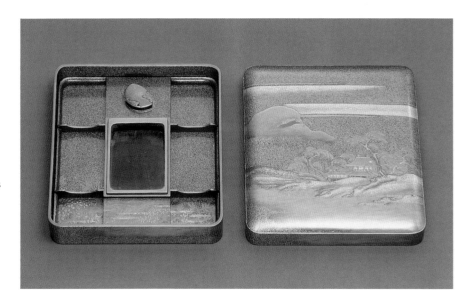

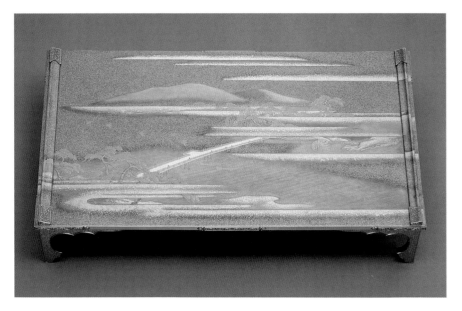

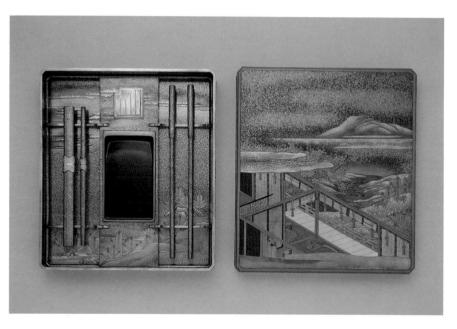

47, 48

Writing case in *maki-e* lacquer

Design of *Hatsune*

Signed Zōhiko
Late Edo Period
26.5 × 24.5 × 4.8 cm
36.5 × 64.5 × 11.4 cm

This shows a scene from an episode *Hatsune* in the *Tale of Genji*. An alternative meaning of *Hatsune* is 'the first child', and this scene was favoured as a decoration for a bride's outfit. The interior of the Rokujō-in temple and its garden with pine and plum trees are painted with gold leaf, coloured lacquer, (vermilion and blue) and in *taka* (high relief) *maki-e* on a lacquer ground, which varies the density. In the open space, pine trees are arranged on the *nashiji* lacquer base. The design on the inkstone case, and a little pitcher placed in the centre, is called *Genji-ko* (perfume of the Genji). This writing case comprises two writing brushes, a little knife and a gimlet. Plum flowers are depicted on the *nashiji* lacquer base. The craftsman, Zohiko, was an active master of *maki-e* in Kyoto during the late Edo and the early Meiji periods.

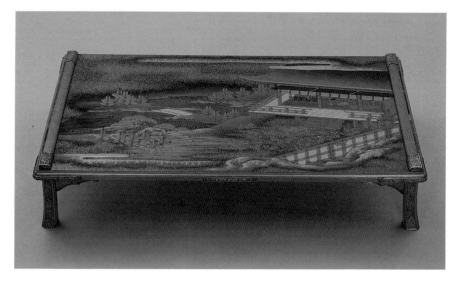

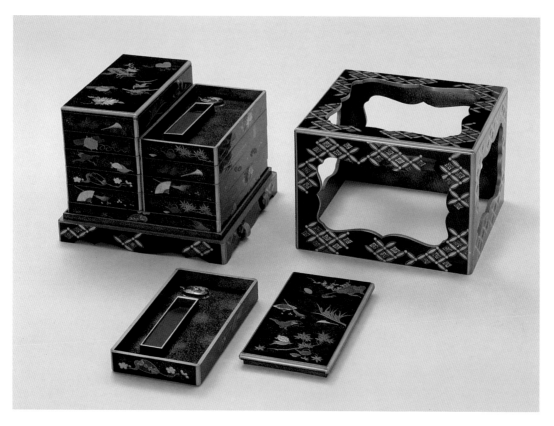

49

Set of writing cases in *maki-e* lacquer
Design of *Kichijo*

Meiji Period
25.3 × 26.5 × 21.5 cm

A stationery set of ten items in two sections and five tiers. On the black-lacquered frame, patterned with gold and silver *maki-e* lacquer is *hanabishi shippo han*, and on the top and the four sides there are five ornamental panels. The writing case itself has a pear-skin lacquer ground decorated in *taka* (high relief) *maki-e* technique with the following lucky symbols: crane, tortoise, moon, toad lily, spool, a military leader's fan, plum tree, bamboo, maple tree.

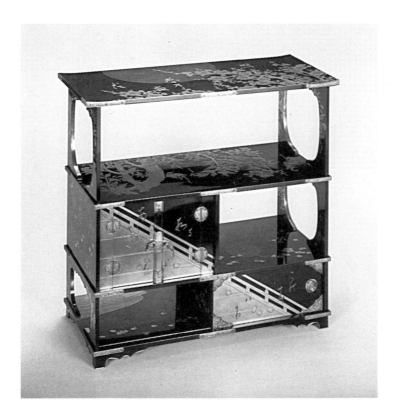

50

Set of shelves

Design of blossom trees and full moon

Mid- to Late Edo Period

32.8 × 71.5 × 65.3 cm

During the Edo period there were three types of shelves included in the dowry of a bride of a feudal lord's family. This type was called *zushi-dana* and used for cosmetics and a stationery case. It is decorated with a spring night scene. A half moon is in polished silver; plum trees, cherry blossoms and a bridge are depicted in *taka* (high relief) *maki-e* on a black-lacquered base. On each side, a poem of Ōe Senri from the *Shin Kokin Waka Shu* (the new edition of the authorized anthology) is inlaid in lead. It reads as follows: 'Nothing is more beautiful than a hazy moon in the vernal night which is not shining nor overcast.'

51

Letter case with crests in *maki-e* lacquer

Edo Period

23.0 × 8.9 × 4.6

A letter case is used to keep or carry letters. On the *nashiji* ground are several family crests including *mitsuba aoi* using gold leaf applied in *taka* (high relief) *maki-e* lacquer technique. The lid is rounded at the corners, and the metal fittings attached on the sides for string are in the shape of a butterfly.

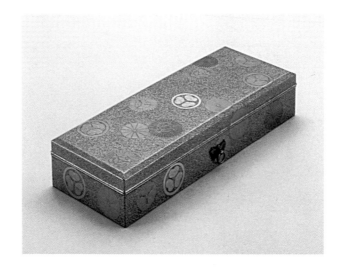

74

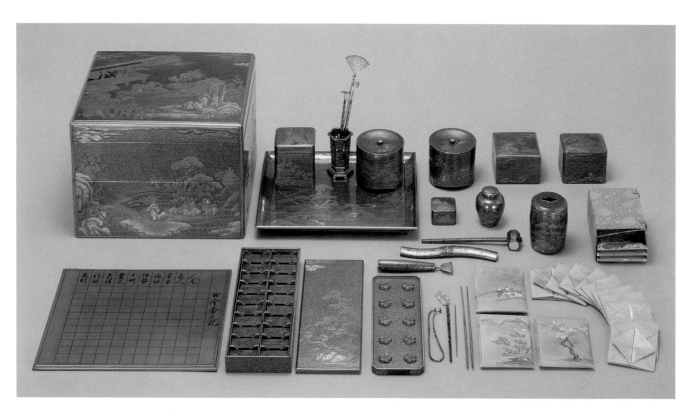

52

Kō–bako (Incense set)

Design of _Hatsune_

Edo Period

21.2 × 24.5 × 18.3 cm

Kōdō is the art of distinguishing the fragrances of burnt incense. The main form of this game is called _kumikō_ which categorizes the several different fragrances mixed according to the subject of a poem or a story. All the aspects of the process of preparing the fragrant incense, burning, smelling and recording, are together called _kō-dogu_ (fragrance tools). Single main pieces, such as a tray, case and incense burner often survive, but this complete 'ten-piece _kōdō_ set' is a rare and important example of lacquer-ware produced in the Edo period.

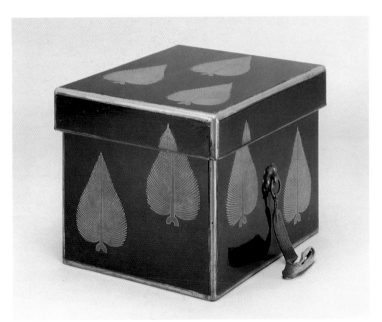

53
Mask case in *maki-e* lacquer
Design of tobacco leaves
Edo Period
28.3 × 23.7 × 21.1 cm

This box is used to keep a mask of a *Nō* or *Kyogen* play. The borders are finished with gold, and on each black-lacquered surface, a few, large tobacco leaves are painted in gold *maki-e* lacquer.

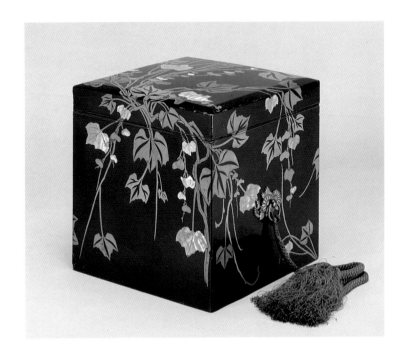

54
Mask case in *maki-e* lacquer
Design of Japanese ivy
Edo Period
22.9 × 22.9 × 23.5 cm

The whole base is lacquered black. On the lid and spilling down the four sides is a design of ivy in gold *maki-e* lacquer, with inlay.

55

Rectangular case with crests in *maki-e* lacquer

Mid- to Late Edo Period

91.6 × 27.3 × 20.8 cm

A pear-skin lacquered ground, varying in density, is decorated with paulownia and arrowhead crests in gold *maki-e* lacquer.

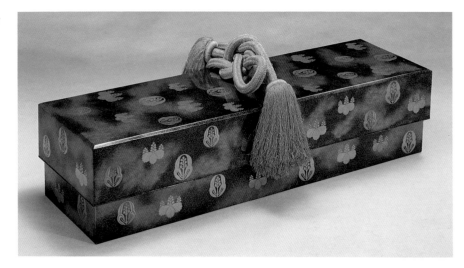

56

Ceremonial headdress stand inlaid in *maki-e* lacquer

Design of chrysanthemums

Mid- to Late Edo Period

27.5 × 35.0 cm

This is said to be a stand for a ceremonial headdress, but its use is not confirmed. The body has five sections of open work. A pattern of chrysanthemums is inlaid in golden *maki-e* lacquer on the top and four sides. The five purple tassels add to the suggestion of opulence.

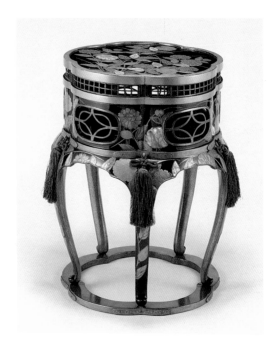

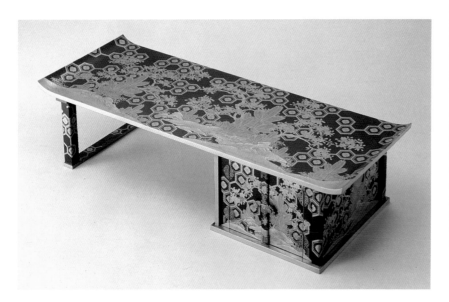

57
Desk in *maki-e* lacquer
Design of cherry blossom, pine needle and tortoiseshell pattern

Late Edo Period
41.0 × 108.0 × 26.0 cm

Kikkō is a pattern of hexagons and literally means the carapace of a tortoise. When the pattern breaks in places, like this one, it is called *yabure kikkō* (torn tortoiseshell). Each end is curved and on the right is a cabinet with double doors. Over the basic *hanabishi kikkō* pattern a clod of earth, cherry blossoms and young pine needles are painted in gold *maki-e*. Although the design is complicated, the total effect is elegant and sophisticated.

58
Hibachi in *maki-e* lacquer
Design of peony, arabesque and hollyhock crest

Late Edo Period
54.5 × 54.5 × 20.8 cm

Hibachi is a heater which burns charcoal. On the *nashiji*-lacquered base, *mitsuba aoi* crests and peonies with arabesques are painted in gold *maki-e*, and crests and arabesques are also carved on the metal fittings.

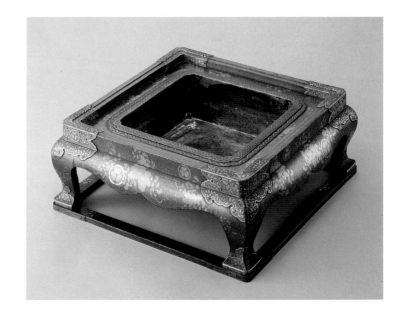

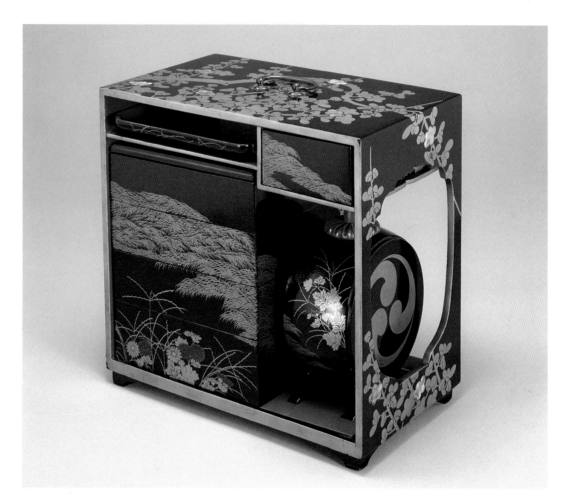

59

Portable luncheon box

Design of flowers

Edo Period

20.0 × 34.0 × 32.0 cm

This is a picnic lunch case devised for outdoor parties under the cherry blossoms. There are two types of picnic case, one a simple set of case with carrier, the other including a *sake* bottle, glasses and dishes. This compact picnic case is of the latter type. The *sake* bottle is, unusually, in shape of a drum. Japanese apricot trees, wild aster and pampas grass are painted in *maki-e* on a black-lacquered base. The apricot flowers are inlaid, and the *sake* bottle is decorated with a large *tomoe* pattern.

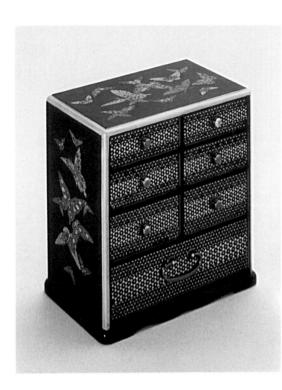

60

Inlaid *Kodansu* (small chest of drawers)

Design of butterfly

Post-Edo

8.8 × 13.8 × 14.3 cm

This inlaid chest is attributed to *Somata* work produced in the Toyama prefecture during the Edo period. The thin mother-of-pearl is finely cut. The reverse side is decorated with applied gold leaf, and the lacquered surface is then inlaid, like mosaic. The front of the drawers is covered with complicated geometrical patterns, while the top and the sides feature a modern butterfly design.

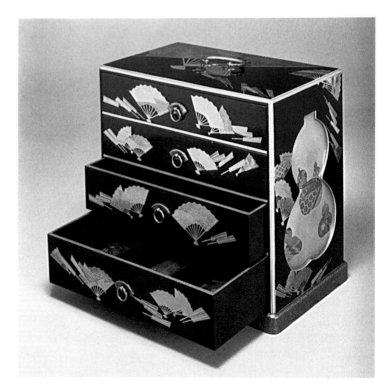

61

***Inrō* cabinet in *maki-e* lacquer**

Design of fan

Post-Edo

17.5 × 29.5 × 28.5 cm

Twelve *inrō*, three per drawer, go in this four-tiered cabinet. Fans are painted in gold and silver *maki-e* on the black-lacquered base. Small gourds are depicted within the larger gold *yokukake*-lacquered gourds on the sides.

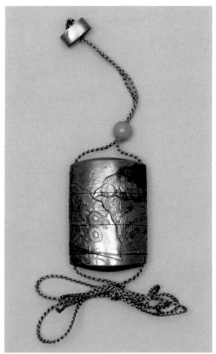

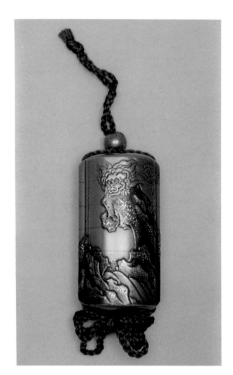

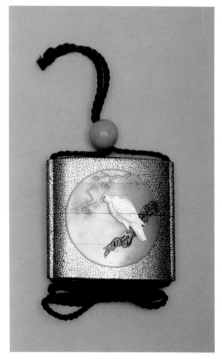

62

Inrō in ***maki-e*** **lacquer**

Design of fan

Signed Kangetsu
Edo Period
5.5 × 4.0 cm

An *inrō* was originally a case for carrying a seal and an inkpad. During the Edo period, its function changed to a portable medicine case. It is usually a flat, four- or five- sectioned case with a string. *Inrō* were designed as small accessories, and they became characteristic of craftwork during the Edo period. Chrysanthemums, cherry flowers, letters and fans decorated with iris are depicted on a gold *yokukake* lacquer ground in *taka* (high relief) *maki-e*. The detail particular to *inrō* work is attractive.

63

Inrō in ***maki-e*** **lacquer**

A scene from *Shakkyo*

Signed Kajikawa
Edo Period
9.0 × 5.4 cm

This five-sectioned medicine case shows a fierce lion with a waterfall on a gold *yokukake* lacquer ground. The design is based on a scene from *Shakkyō*, a *Nō* play episode. This theme often appears in paintings and textiles. The lion in gold *maki-e* covering the *inro* gives a rich and powerful impression. The Kajikawa is the *maki-e* craftsman-in-ordinary to the Tokugawa shogunate, from the time Kajikawa Hikobei served the Tokugawa during the Kambun period (1661–73). The Kajikawa excelled at *inrō* work in elaborate *maki-e* lacquer. The rich effect of this piece is typical.

64

Inrō in ***maki-e*** **lacquer**

Design of pine tree and eagle

Signed Shibayama
Mid- to Late Edo Period
8.2 × 7.5 cm

This three-sectioned case is decorated with a circle featuring an eagle on a pine tree. The *taka* (high relief) *maki-e* lacquer technique is used to depict the pine tree, while lightly-carved mother-of-pearl is used to represent the eagle. Outside the circle *hirame* textile creates a thick flake-like surface. Shibayama originates from the place in the Shimōsa Province (present Chiba prefecture) where Onogi Senzō (later Shibayama Senzō) devised an inlay work with mother-of-pearl and ivory, around the An'ei period (1772–81). The technique was called 'Shibayama work'.

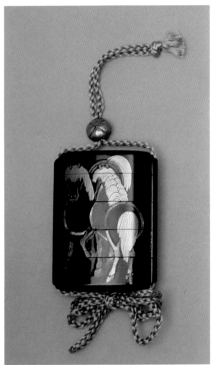

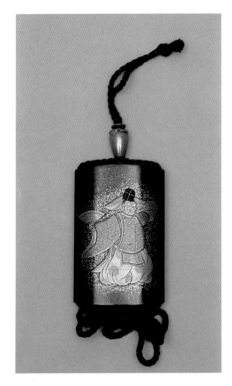

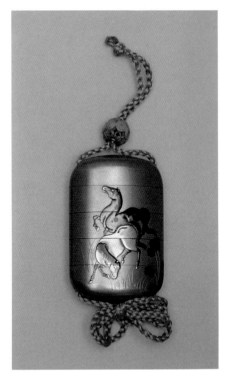

65

***Inrō* with inlay in *maki-e* lacquer**

Design of horse

Signature and seal of Shiomi Masanari
Early Edo Period
8.0 × 7.0 cm

The case has four sections. Horses are outlined with inlay, the mane and tail depicted in *togidashi maki-e*, a lacquer technique using a polished sprinkled design. The artist, Shiomi Masanari (1646–1719), was a noted Kyoto specialist in this technique. In contrast to the fashion of that time, his style was graceful and sophisticated. The works were named after him and called 'Shiomi *maki-e*'. His descendants followed him in his profession. This piece is a good example of his simple and refined style.

66

***Inrō* in *maki-e* lacquer**

Design from a *Noh* play

Signature and seal of Yūtokusai
Late Edo Period
8.0 × 5.6 cm

On this four-sectioned medicine case, a *Nō* performer in costume is depicted in *taka* (high relief) *maki-e*, a decorative technique mixing lacquer and powder. The pear-skin lacquer ground effectively expresses the symbolic nature of the *Nō* play. Yūtokusai was one of the noted masters of *inrō* work in the late Edo period.

67

***Inrō* in *maki-e* lacquer**

Design of horse

Signed Shōkasai
Edo Period
8.0 × 6.0 cm

On this four-sectioned oval-shaped medicine case, three horses are depicted on one side and two on the other in gold and silver powder mixed with black lacquer. Each horse's action, colours and patterns are different, and the varying lie of the hair is attractive. The appeal of the horses is the focus of the simple decoration.

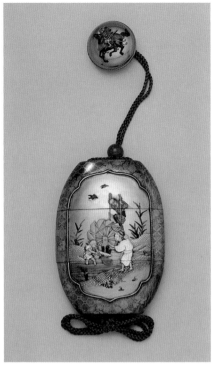
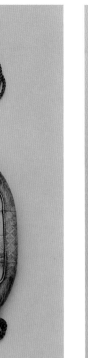
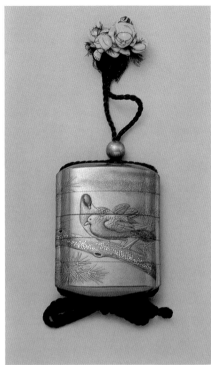
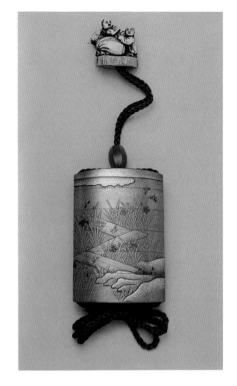

68

Inrō with inlay in _maki-e_ lacquer

Design of watermill and arranged flowers

Signed Shibayama

Post-Edo Period

12.4 × 9.0 cm

This is a large two-sectioned medicine case with an oval on each surface. Around it, _shippohan_ technique is applied. On the _tachioke_ ground, a crest of paulownia is depicted in _hira_ (relief) _maki-e_ lacquer. Inside the panels, a watermill and a figure are painted on one side, and on the other white chrysanthemums arranged in a vase, executed in dyed ivory, horn and inlaid shell with _taka maki-e_. The skilful inlay work is attributed to Shibayama work, produced after the Meiji period.

69

Inrō in _maki-e_ lacquer

Design of pine tree and pigeon (Reverse illustrated on page 17)

Post-Edo Period

10.2 × 8.1 cm

This four-sectioned medicine case is decorated with two pigeons on a branch of a pine tree in gold and silver powders with _taka_ (high relief) _maki-e_ technique on a gold _yokukake_ base. The finely ground gold leaf is sprinkled over the pine branches. The careful but natural figures of the two pigeons are appealing.

70

Inrō in _maki-e_ lacquer

Design of _Yatsuhashi_

Post-Edo Period

10.5 × 7.4 cm

Yatsuhashi, the subject of this five-sectioned medicine case, is a place noted for its beautiful _kakitsubata_ (rabbit-ear iris) flowers. It is described in the ninth episode (entitled 'Narihira Azuma Kudari no Jō' of the _Ise Monogatari_ (Ise Short Stories). A bridge, iris flowers and fireflies are depicted in _taka_ (high relief) _maki-e_ lacquer technique, with the lightning part of the firefly represented by inlaid mother-of-pearl.

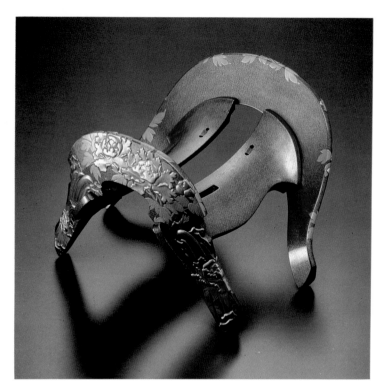

71, 72

***Abumi* and *kura* (Stirrups and saddle)**

Design of peony flower and waterfall in *maki-e* lacquer

Late Edo Period

27.5 × 26.2 × 36.3 cm

36.0 × 41.5 × 27.5 cm

A *kura* is a saddle for a cow or a horse, used for a rider or baggage. It is made either of wood, leather or metal. *Abumi* are stirrups with metal fittings. The saddle is composed of three parts to which decoration is applied. In this example the base is decorated in *tsumenashi* lacquer and Nunobiki waterfall and peony flowers are depicted in a rich *taka* (high relief) *maki-e* technique on the front and the back. Cut gold leaf has been applied to the centre of the flower. In the late Edo period, when no major battles took place, this type of impractical, decorative harness was produced, called the *daimyo dōgu* (a luxurious outfit for feudal lords).

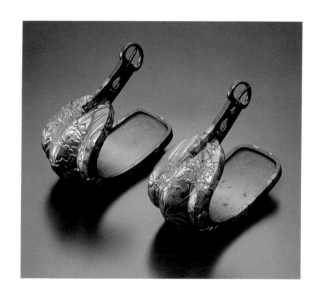

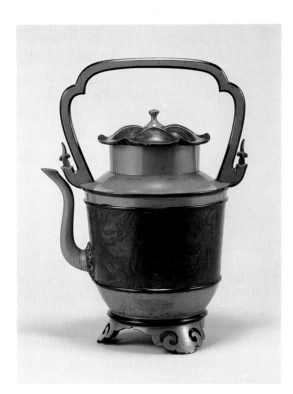

73

Jug for hot water

Negoro lacquer

Edo Period

19.8 × 27.9 × 35.7 cm

Lacquer-ware with a black undercoat and vermilion topcoat is generally called *Negoro* lacquer. It is said that the name *Negoro* has its origin in the fact that vermilion-lacquered daily table-ware was used at the Negoro Temple in Kishū Province in the Muromachi period from the end of the 13th to the late 16th century. The same technique seems to be applied to lacquer-ware produced in various places in more recent times. Most of the *Negoro* lacquer-ware is functional. The simple shape and clear tone, combining beauty and utility are characteristic. The black-lacquered undercoat is partly exposed, due to the vermilion topcoat wearing out. The shape is Chinese and the style is distinctively foreign.

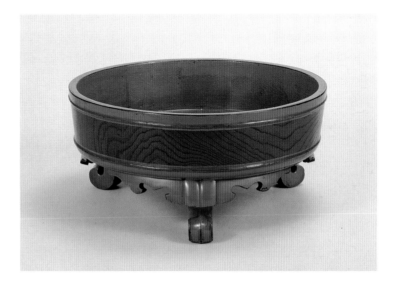

74

Basin with legs

Negoro lacquer

Momoyama Period

36.4 × 16.8 cm

This is commonly called a horse tub, but the original use was for washing hands. The lacquered body is carved from *keyaki* (uzelkova) wood and has four legs.

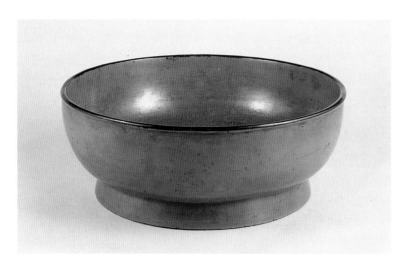

75

***Maru-bachi* (bowl)**

Negoro lacquer

Muromachi Period

39.0 × 14.5 cm

The shape is simple and plain, while the body line is dynamic and forceful. This is a masterpiece of *Negoro* lacquer-ware which dates back to the Muromachi period.

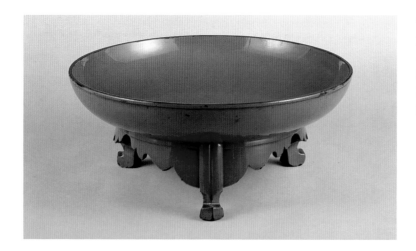

76

Bowl with legs

Negoro lacquer

Edo Period

34.9 × 13.9 cm

Lacquered wood

77
Soup bowls (*wan*)

Edo Period
14.4 × 10.5 cm
13.9 × 7.3 cm

Lacquered wood

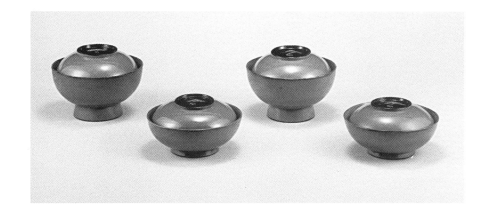

78
Soup bowls (*wan*)

Edo Period
12.3 × 9.1 cm

Lacquered wood, with chrysanthemum and abstract design

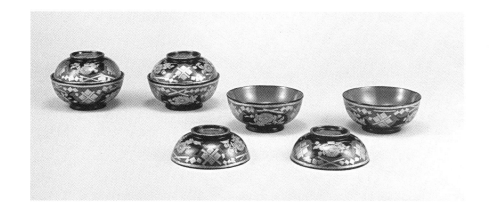

79
Soup bowls (*wan*)

Edo Period
10.9 × 12.6 cm

Lacquered wood, with chrysanthemum and abstract design

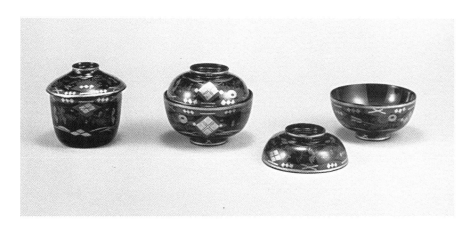

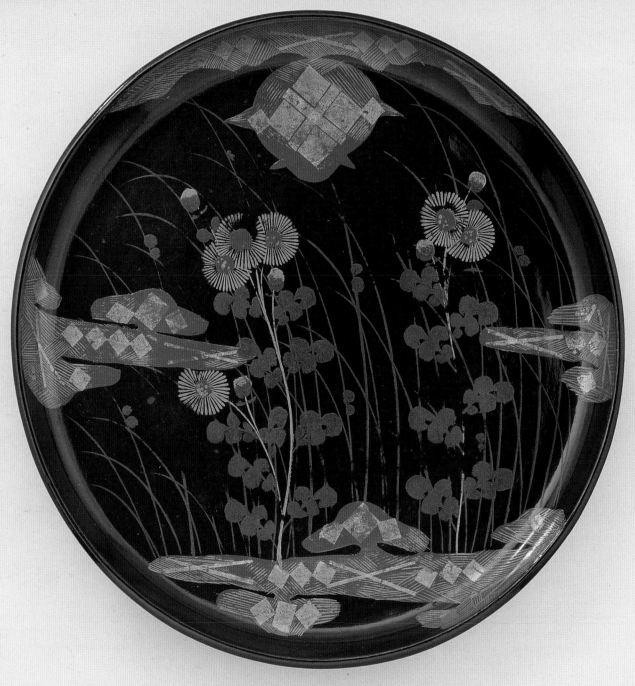

80

Tray (*bon*)

Edo Period

29.8 × 5.3 cm

Lacquered wood, with chrysanthemum and abstract design

81

Tray (*bon*)

Edo Period

37.6 × 3.5 cm

Lacquered wood, with iris design in *maki-e* decoration

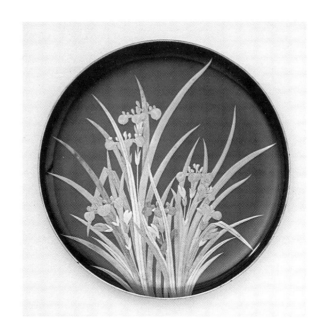

82

Trays (*bon*)

Early Edo Period

37.5 × 4.1 cm

Lacquered wood, with flower and vine design

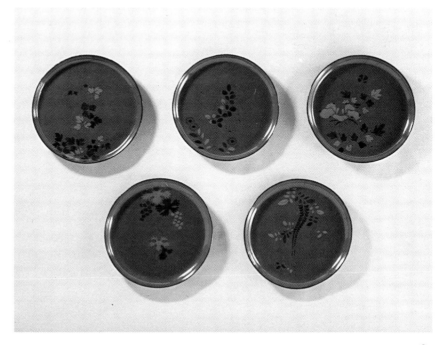

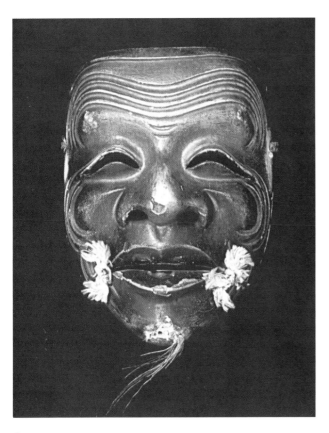

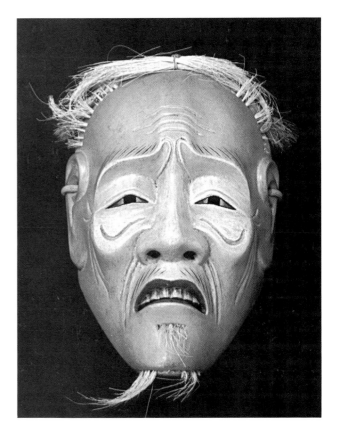

83

Kyogen **mask**

Representing *Kokushiki-Jo*, Old Black Man

Edo Period

19.0 × 15.0 × 8.5 cm

Painted wood

84

Nō **mask**

Representing *Jō*, Old Man

Edo Period

21.0 × 15.2 × 7.8 cm

85

Nō **mask**

Representing *Ōtobide*, Devil with ferocious grin

Edo Period

23.2 × 18.1 × 9.5 cm

Painted wood

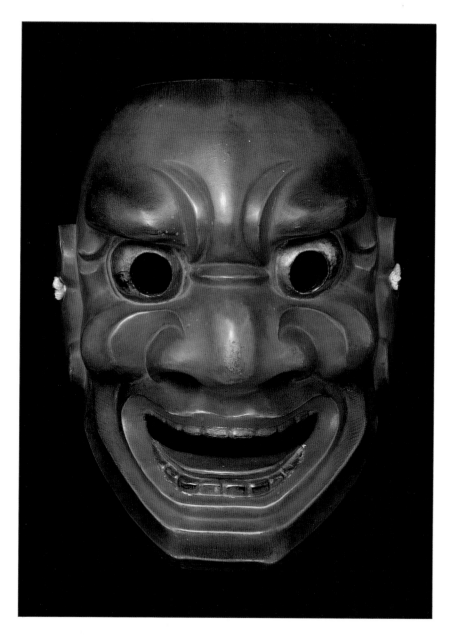

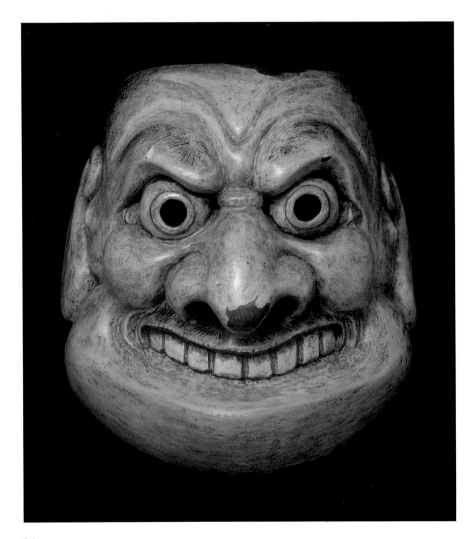

86

Kyogen **mask**

Representing *Buaku*, Comic Devil

Edo Period

19.4×15.0×9.7 cm

ARMS AND ARMOUR

87

Suit of armour in the Ōyoroi style

Edo Period
Height 160.3 cm

Iron, decorated with lacquer, leather and silk
lacing

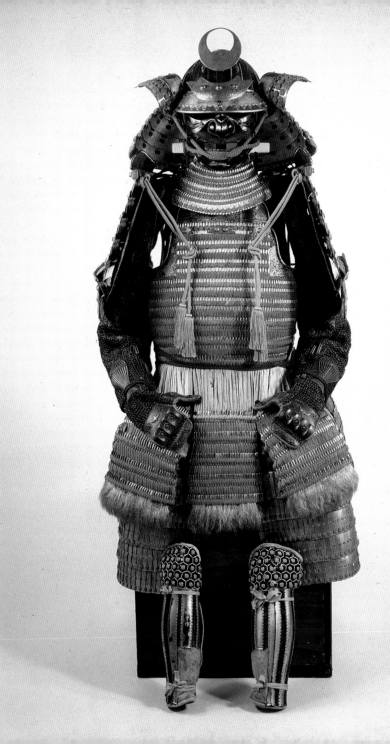

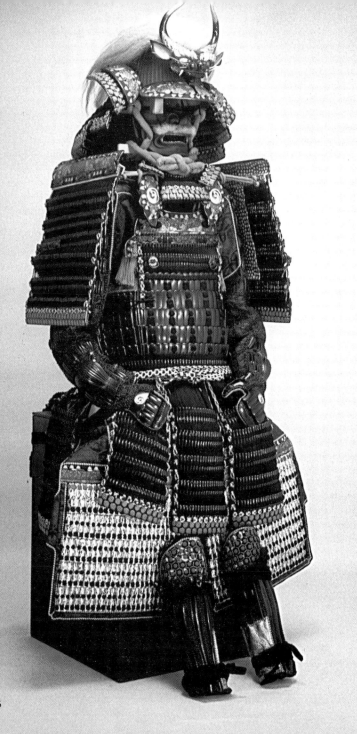

88

Suit of armour in *Gomaidō Gusoku* style

Attributed to Oguri Kōzukenosuke
Late Edo Period
Height 168.0 cm

Gusoku originally meant 'completeness' and 'sufficiency'. During the prosperous feudal times, the word came to indicate a style of fully-equipped armour. This *gusoku*, a majestic masterpiece of the late Edo period, is attributed to Oguri Kōzukenosuke. The black *kozane* (a plate made of iron or leather) and the dark blue laces, which are the major parts of this armour, look solid. The gold, used in the *kusazuri* (leg-protector) and *maedate* (an accessory attached to the front of helmet), gives an impression of richness. The details are finely and elaborately worked.

89

Suit of armour in *Okegawa* style

Used by the Tōdō family
Edo Period
Height 172.0 cm

Kittsuke kozane (small material plates) are laced
with indigo blue cord. On the black-lacquered
plastron, joined sideways, a dragon with cloud
is depicted in gold *taka* (high relief) *maki-e*.
The shoulder part of the arm protector bears a
sign and the side parts of the helmet and
bracelets are decorated with ivy. The ivy is the
traditional crest of the head family of Tōdō,
which suggests that this showy feudal lord's
equipment was used by a member of the Tōdō
family. The maker of this helmet is Suifuki
Yoshinori, an ordinary craftsman of the
Tokugawa shogunate in the Mito Province.
He was one of the Myōchin school masters,
and awarded a Chinese character, *yoshi*, from
the feudal chief, Nariaki. He became a
professional armour-maker.

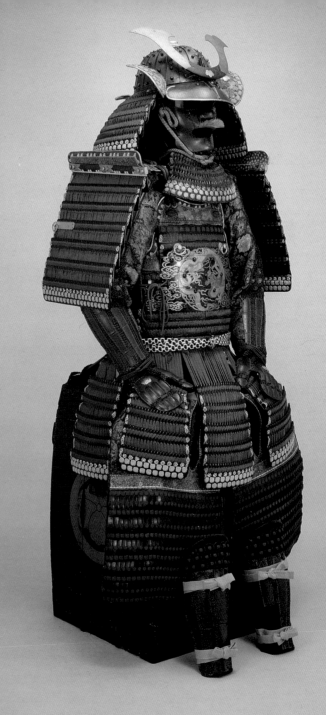

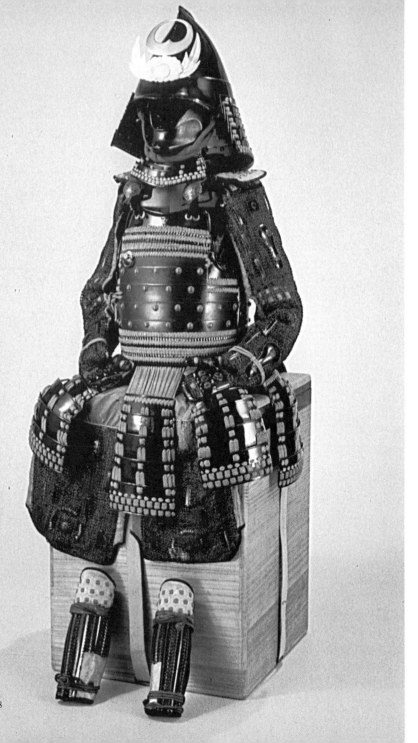

90

**Suit of armour for a child, in *Nimaidō
Gusoku* style**

Edo Period
Height 160.0 cm

Iron, decorated with lacquer, leather and silk
lacing

91

Honkozane armour in *Dōmaru* style

Edo Period
Height 169.0 cm

Iron, decorated with lacquer, leather and silk
lacing

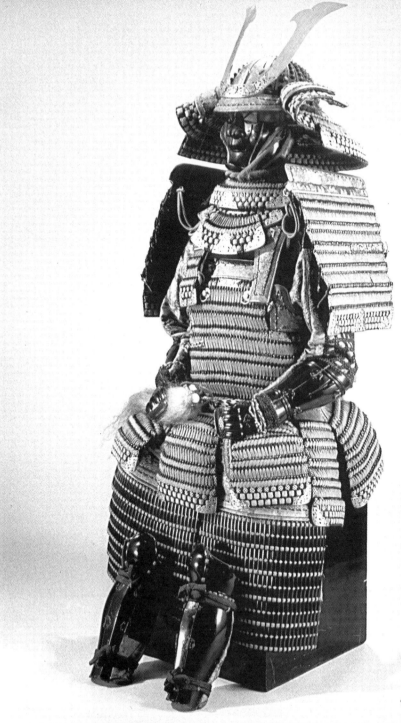

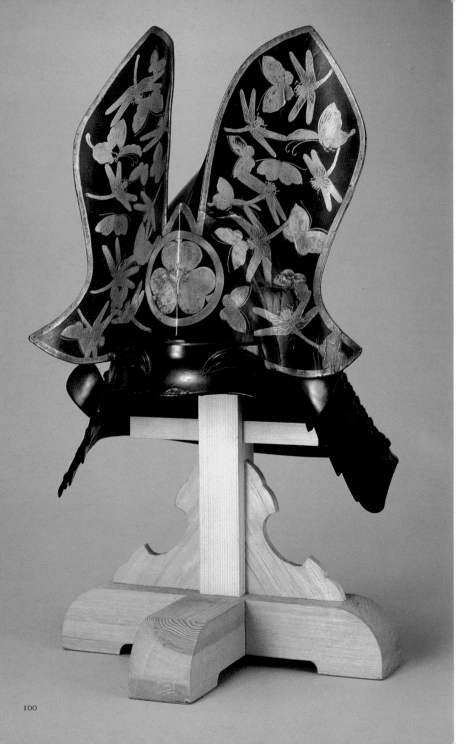

92

Harikake fancy helmet with the crest of the Tokugawas

Believed to have been used by the Tokugawa Ieyasu
Momoyama Period
32.0 × 32.0 × 40.0 cm

From the end of the Muromachi period many different designs were used for armour and helmets. _Harikake_ is a method of modelling an abstract or figurative motif by covering piled-up Japanese papers with lacquer. The _harikake_ helmets produced in the Edo period were of exquisite workmanship. A pattern of dragon-flies and butterflies in _hira_ (relief) _maki-e_ surrounds the central _mitsuba aoi_, a family crest of the Tokugawas. It is said that the then shogun, Tokugawa Ieyasu, used this helmet.

93

Sixty-two *ken suji* helmet

Signed Jōshū Jū Saotome Ienari
Momoyama Period
33.0 × 31.0 × 17.5 cm

The *suji* helmet is in a style dating from the early 14th century and into the Muromachi period. Little pieces of thin, rectangular iron plates are joined by small rivets with flattened heads which show only the *suji* (joins) of those plates. The name 'sixty-two *ken*' (sixty-two spaces) comes from the number of plates used. The *shikoro* (neck guard) is laced in *sugake* pattern with indigo blue cords. *Mitsu-kashiwa*, a patrimonial family crest of the Makinos, is put on each *fukikaeshi* (side part). It is ornamented with a large crescent made from dressed leather on which gold leaf is pressed. The craftsman, Saotome Ienari, who lived in the Jōshū Province (present Ibaraki prefecture) was the third head of the Saotome school which was active from the end of the Muromachi to the Momoyama period. *Suji* helmets, like this one, were his favourite subject and many of his works are large in contrast to others of the Saotome.

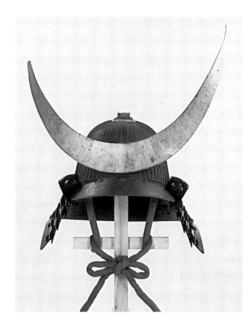

94

Sixty-two *ken suji* helmet

Signed Saotome Iechika
Momoyama Period
34.0 × 34.0 × 16.0 cm

This helmet is made from 62 riveted plates. The craftsman, Saotomo Iechika, produced many splendid helmets in a generally restrained style. These are well-forged with almost flat tops and oval at the bottom, with deep crowns. The gold-lacquered *shikoro* (neck guard) is laced with ancient-purple cord with *kittsuke kozane* plates. The sides are ornamented with a pair of carved wooden antlers on which gold leaf is applied. The *rokumon-sen* (six-*mon* coins) pattern on the *fukikaeshi* (side part), indicates that this helmet belonged to the Sanadas, the ruling family (with a fief yielding 120,000 *koku*) of the Castle of Matsushiro in the Shinshū Province (the present Nagano prefecture).

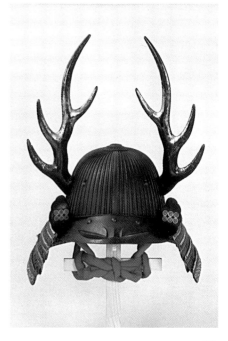

95

Helmet in *Namban* style with visor

Momoyama Period
36.0 × 35.0 27.0 cm

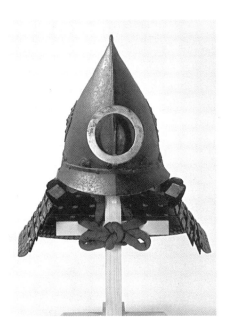

The types of helmets produced from the late Muromachi period onward include *zunari*, *momonari* and *eboshinari*. The *momonari* (peach-shaped) was influenced by the Namban style and has a ridge running back from the middle of the front with the right and left sides smooth so as to deflect blows. This is a representative example of that particular type in the Momoyama period. Rather than shaping a single piece of iron, four pieces were used to form this helmet. The black-lacquered *shikoro* (neck plate) is laced with grass-green threads, making six lines in *hinone* pattern. The *fukikaeshi* (side parts) have the *hanabishi* crest in gold, while the front is ornamented with a *janome* crest, a wooden ring covered with gold.

96

Harikake helmet in Chinese style

Edo Period
30.0 × 30.0 × 27.0 cm

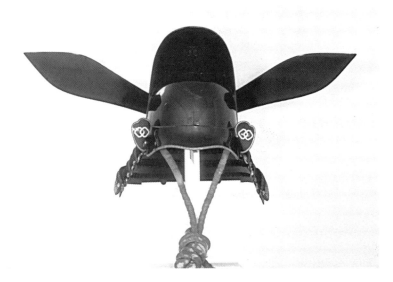

From the late Muromachi period helmet designs showed considerable variety. The most common design, a cap or crown modelled, like this one, on a Chinese headdress, was popular in the Momoyama period. Thin iron, dressed leather and lacquered *washi* (Japanese paper) are attached to a plain *zunari* helmet. The ear-shaped blades, attached to the back, function as *tatemono* (ornaments to flaunt power). The simplified *fukikaeshi* (side parts) carry the *tagaisumikiri* (rounded-off square) crests in gold.

97

Tenkokusannari helmet

Edo Period
37.0 × 37.0 × 30.0 cm

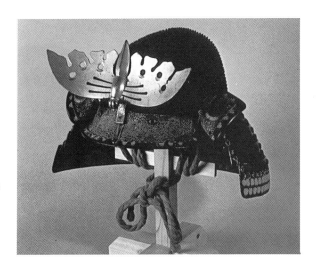

The helmets produced during the Edo period are individually called: *ō-boshi*, *chu-boshi* and *ko-boshi* (large, middle and small stars) according to the size of the rivets. These sizes are not categorized by exact measurements, so attribution depends on the visual image. Judging from the size of rivets, this helmet, typical work of the Myōchin school in the Edo period, can reasonably be identified as *ko-boshi* (little stars). It is also called *tenkokusannari* (hollowed-top). It is ornamented with a butterfly, carved in wood covered with gold leaf. *Kara-hana* (Chinese flower) crests are on the *fukikaeshi* (side parts) and lions with arabesques are symmetrically arranged on the right and left of the visor.

98

Sōmempō (Face guard)

Mid-Edo Period
36.0 × 27.5 × 15.0 cm

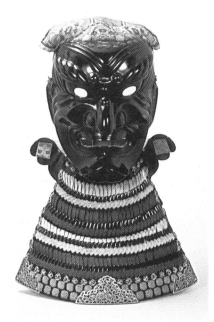

A *sōmempō* is a full face guard. These began to be made at the time of the Nambokucho (southern and northern Imperial Courts, 1333–92). They were not as popular as *hōate* (half-mask), and most of them were made to show off the master craftsman's skill in the Edo period. This elaborate work is an example. The whole face is of black-lacquered dressed *nerikawa* leather, with the collar-flap laced in *honkozane* pattern with purple threads. The *fukikaeshi* (side parts) are patterned with the gold Chinese character, '*dai*' which means 'magnificence', 'prosperity' and 'strong power'.

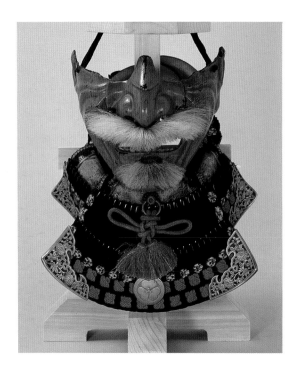

99

Shirohige *ressei–mempō* (Face guard)

Edo Period

33.0×27.0×17.0 cm

A *ressei-mempō* is a style of half-mask with a
furious and threatening facial expression.
Other characteristics are the wrinkled nose and
cheeks, the widely opened mouth, the beard
and moustache, and the gold teeth. This work,
a typical vermilion-lacquered *ressei-mempō*, has
the *guruwa* (collar) often attached to the face
guards produced in the Edo period. The
katabami (oxalis), favoured as a family crest by
military commanders in a turbulent age, is
worked with gold in the centre below the
collar-flap.

100

Abumi (stirrups) in *hira* (relief) *maki-e*

Signed *Gashu-jū Masahira Saku* (Made by
Masahira in Gashu)

Edo Period

27.0×13.3×25.0 cm

Abumi is a pair of stirrups suspended from each
side of a saddle for the rider's feet. The
signature indicates that this pair was made by
Masahira, a craftsman of Iga Abumi, who lived
in the Gashu Province (the western part of the
present Mie prefecture) around the mid-Edo
period. On the outside, butterflies and
arabesques are elaborately inlaid in silver on the
rusted iron. On the black-lacquered inside,
gold and silver butterflies are depicted in *hira
maki-e*. The decorative style is typical of the
Edo period.

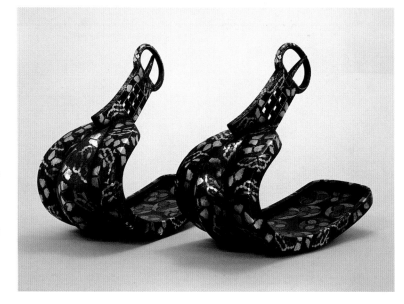

101

Matchlock pistol

Mid-Edo Period
Length 25.5 cm

In the peaceful mid-Edo period, target shooting with firelocks in private gardens was a popular pastime. The body of this firelock is elaborately inlaid with silver. The *mitsuba* crest carved near the muzzle commemorates the success of a legitimate son of the Tokugawas in the Kyōhō period (about 1730) of the mid-Edo. This is one of a few surviving masterpieces and was also used as a room ornament.

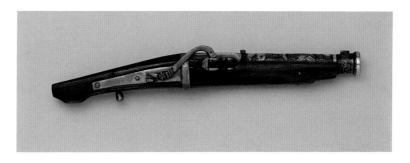

102

Military fan

Late Edo Period
36.5 × 64.0 cm

It was a traditional custom for a warrior to bring a fan with him to his military base. Several of these fans are described in the famous war chronicles, for example *The Tale of Heike*. In addition to their use as fans, they were also used to give commands and signals, and to indicate a warrior's status. Because of its military use, the fan's structure is solid, with 13 black-lacquered wooden sticks. A large vermilion disc, symbolizing the rising sun, is painted on the gold-leafed obverse, while on the reverse side a gold disc is painted on vermilion lacquer.

103

Jutte

Signed Sadatsugu Saku (made by Sadatsugu)
Mid-Edo Period
Length 42.5 cm

Jutte is an iron tool about 45cm long, used to
deflect an attacker's blade or to make an attack
while arresting a criminal. The colour of the
tassels attached to the haft indicate its owner's
post or station. Among those which survive,
there are few bearing a signature, particularly
on the haft. This sword type is so rare that it
probably did not belong to an ordinary officer,
but was commissioned from a craftsman by a
senior official. The signature indicates that it
was made by a swordsmith, Sadatsugu, who
was active in the mid–Edo period.

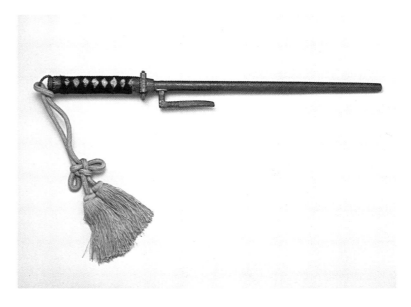

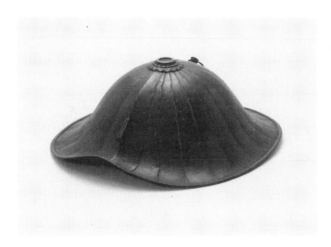

104

Jingasa, **military hat**

Signed Myōchin Munenori
Mid-Edo Period
33.0 × 28.0 × 12.0 cm

During the civil wars, common soldiers put on
jingasa hats instead of helmets. These were
usually made of iron or leather and lacquered.
In the Edo period, a shogun and his vassals
wore the black-lacquered *jingasa* with a gold
crest in the field. In this example 24 pieces of
thin iron plates are joined together with seven
rivets. It faithfully copies the style of military
hats from more turbulent times. It is attributed
to Myōchin Munenori (the years of his birth
and death are unknown), who probably lived
in the mid-Edo period.

105

Jimbaori, surcoat

Edo Period
88.0 × 50.8 cm

A soldier put on a *jimbaori*, which is generally sleeveless, over his armour when in camp. It is said the style copied the clothes of Spaniards or Portuguese who came to Japan in the Muromachi period. The material is white silk, the front ornamented with a pattern. From the *Myōga-mon*, a family crest of the Nabeshimas in the Bizen Province (present Saga prefecture), it is assumed that a warrior related to the Nabeshima family wore this surcoat.

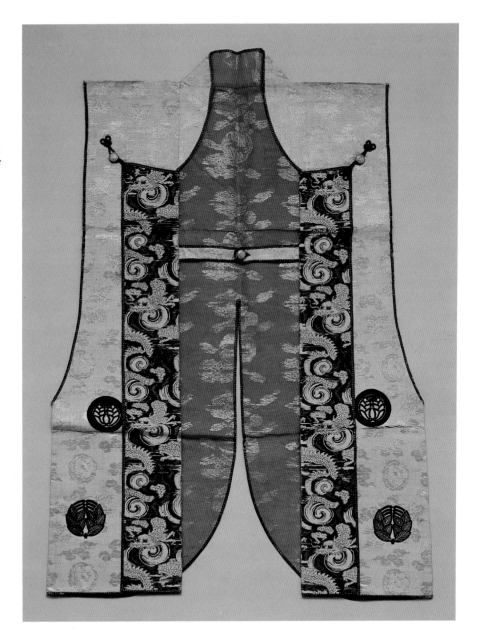

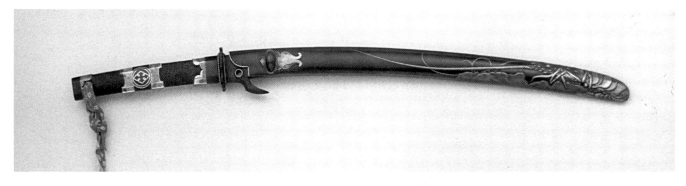

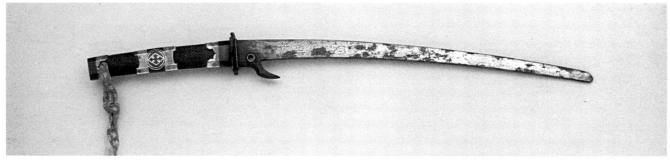

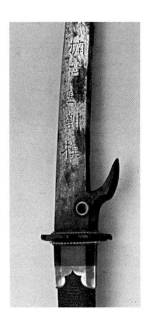
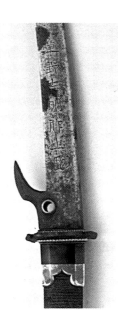

106

Hachiwari, crown chopper

Signed (obverse) *Kusunoki Ko Hachiwari Mo* (copied Kusino Ko's crown chopper), (reverse) *Kusano Yoshiaki Saku* (seal) (made by Kusano Yoshiaki)
Total length 52.0 cm, blade 34.0 cm

A *hachiwari* is a weapon used to break an enemy's helmet. It looks like a *jutte* (common officer's protective weapon) with a haft and a sheath. It is said that Kusunoki Masanari was the first to order and use it on the battlefield. From the signature, this can be attributed to Kusano Yoshiaki, who belonged to Gassan Sadayoshi's school in Osaka in the late Edo period. It is a copy of Kusunoki Ko's crown chopper. A lobster is elaborately worked in *taka* (high relief) *maki-e* on the tip of the sheath. This is one of the few examples that has survived.

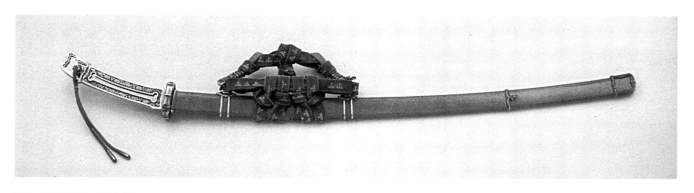

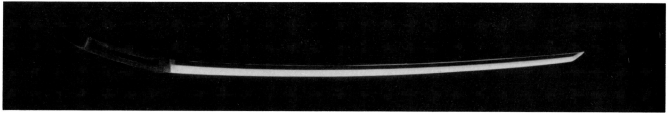

107

Tachi **sword in the shape of tweezers**

Unsigned
Late Edo Period
Total length 88.0 cm, blade 70.5 cm

This is a type of sword produced in a period of transition, when the shape was changing from straight to curved. It is characterized by an opening in the haft which functions to reduce the damage given by cutting. This is a copy of the sword in a collection of the Ise shrine, and is believed to have belonged to Fujiwara-no Hidesato, a powerful clan in Shimotsuke during the mid-Heian period. Its minute patterns and carvings on the metal fittings are faithful to the original. The blade is attributed to Kawai Hisayuki, a swordsmith in the Musashi Province in the late Edo period. The blade curves sharply into the hilt, which is characteristic of this type of sword, and accurately reproduced. This is a particularly important piece as there are few existing originals or copies.

108

Katana **sword**

Signed (reverse) Masatsune (illustrated on page 18)
Heian Period (about 1027-37)
Total length 77.0 cm, blade 62.0 cm

The Bigo Province is famous for its production of swords. In the late Heian, the oldest period of manufacturing Japanese swords, a group called the Kobizen School was formed, and Masatsune was noted as a representative master in the school. It is said that there were a number of swordsmiths called Masatsune at this time. Judging from its style, this probably belongs to the Kobizen school. The *sinogi* (longitudinal ridge between the edge and the back, usually closer to the back) is attached to both sides of the blade, one of which is sharp edged. The *iori mune*, opposite the cutting edge, is narrow-bladed and slightly curved. The pattern along the sharp edge is *Komine*. The ridge line and ornamentation of this sword give it a characteristic traditional elegance.

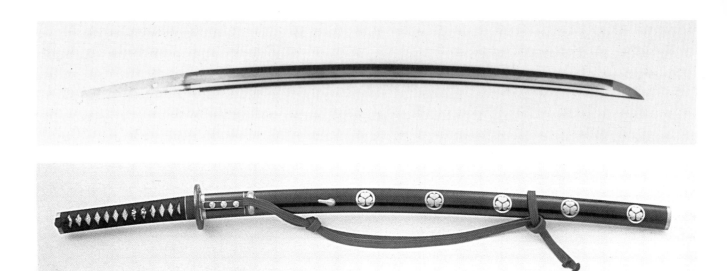

109

Katana sword

Signed Hioki Tsushima Myudō Chikyu
Tsunemitsu
Early Edo Period
Total length 94.2 cm, blade 72.0 cm

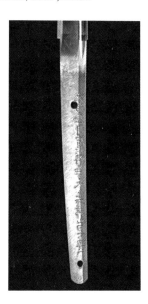

Tsunemitsu was born in Gamō in the Kōshū
Province, and moved with his younger
brother, Mitsuhira, to Yotsuya in Edo. He
called himself Hioki Ichinojo and
Saburozaemon. After becoming a Buddhist lay
priest, he changed his name to Ippō. Ishidō
Sakon Zeich, his brother Mitsuhira, and
Tsunemitsu are representative swordsmiths of
the Edo Ishido school. There is another sword,
bearing the same signature as this and also the
figure 73 (1698), which is attributed to
Tsunemitsu's later years. This sword character-
izes his style of blade – Ichimonji Utsushi. The
fittings are black-lacquered and bear an *A-oi*
crest in gold *maki-e*. From the family crest on
the sheath and fittings, this sword seems to be
associated with the Tokugawa shogunate. Its
excellent condition suggests that a noble feudal
family must have carefully preserved it.

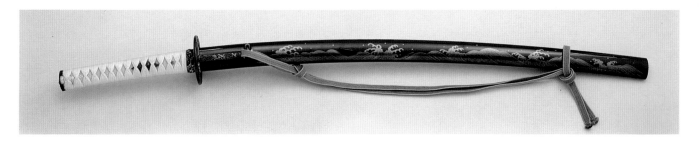

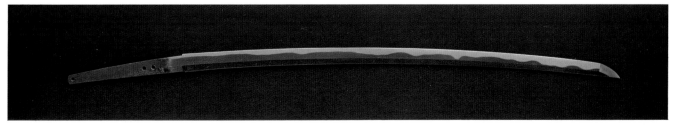

Katana sword

Inscribed (obverse) *Etchu no kami Fujiwara no Takahira*, (reverse) *Genna Hachi-nen Go-gatsu* (5th mth, 8th yr, Genwa era, 1622)
Total length 94.0 cm, blade 74.5 cm

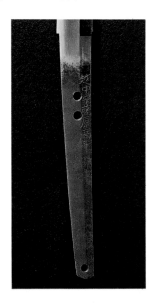

Takahira was an active master craftsman in Kaga Province, which is a part of the present Ishikawa prefecture, from the Momoyama to early Edo period. This is the longest and the finest sword among his works. The steel is well forged, showing *itamehada* texture. The wavy edge pattern is called *gunome*, and these are tiny *nioi awa* grains toward the *shinogi* (longitudinal ridge). The *koshirae* (*katana* fittings) include a sheath finished in gold *maki-e* lacquer with a wavy design on black lacquer, a haft with braided *unohana* on white sharkskin, and a guard on which a battle scene at the Uji river is carved.

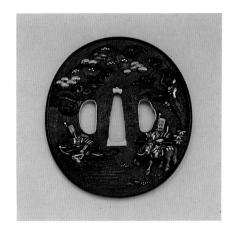

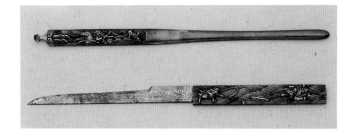

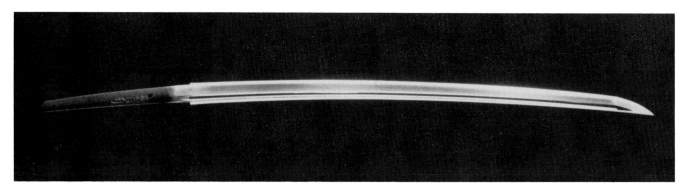

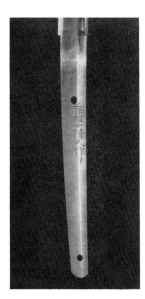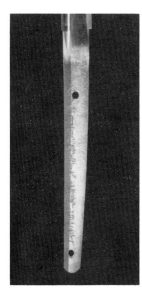

III

Katana **sword**

Inscribed (obverse) *Fujiwara no Kyondo Saku* (made by Fujiwara no Kyondo), (reverse) *Genji Gan-nen Jyūgatsu-yokka* (1st yr, Genji Era, Late Edo period, 1864)
Total length 88.0 cm, blade, 72.0 cm

The swordsmith was a student of Minamoto no Kiyomaro who was regarded as the greatest master in the late Edo period. He was born in Shōnai district (north-western part of Yamagata prefecture), moved to Edo (present Tokyo), becoming a disciple of Kiyomaro and followed his artistic style. In 1867, he went to Bizen Province (between present Fukuoka and Ōita prefectures) to study sword-making. Later he returned and concentrated on forging swords until 1901 when he died. The period of his production can be divided into three stages, Edo, Bizen and Dewa. This example was made in 1864, the end of the Edo period. He produced two different types of work, 'Kiyomaro style' and 'Yamato Province style'. This example belongs to the latter. It is finely textured, in the *suguha* style, curving slightly from the *nakago* (haft) toward the large *kissaki* (point) with striking beauty.

Glossary

Abumi – Stirrups.

Ama-no-hashidate – A sandbar in Miyatsu Bay in Miyatsu city, Kyoto. One of the 'Three Views of Japan'. It is especially famous for the three kilometres of white sand and pine forest.

Bon – Tray, with or without small feet.

Bundai – A small writing table approximately 10cm high, with a rectangular top used for books etc, from the Heian period. A smaller version was used at poetry recitals. In the Muromachi period the *Bundai* was made with an inkstone box. In the Edo period it was considered to be one of a feudal lord's essential accessories.

Byōbu – Screen of from two to eight hinged panels, used as a room divider. Introduced to Japan from China during the 8th century, at Nara. They were decorated with paintings, the four seasons and landscapes being favourite themes.

Fubako – A box in which letters were kept.

Fusuma – Sliding doors, composed of a wooden frame covered on both sides with thick paper or fabric. Frequently decorated with paintings or calligraphy, they were used as interior partitions.

Genji-monogatari (The Tale of Genji) – Written in the Heian period (the beginning of the 11th century) by Murasaki Shikibu. It is a love-story, describing life at court and the vivid adventures of the hero, Prince Genji, and the many women with whom he was involved. It consists of 54 volumes. There were many '*Genji-e*' (*Genji* pictures) picturing the main scenes of the tale. These scenes, painted in various forms on picture scrolls, folding screens and lacquer-work, became universal and classic themes in Japanese art.

Gomaidō – *Gomaidō* are the five hinged sections which make up the cuirass of *gosuku* armour, a new type developed in the latter half of the 16th century. *Nimaidō* refers to a cuirass with only two hinged sections, *go* meaning five and *ni*, two. The sections could be made of large sheets of hammered iron, tiers of lames or long horizontal panels.

Hamon – Patterns along the sharp edge of a sword blade.
Swords are often admired for the straight or irregular patterns which define the hard-tempered edge. Before the sword was handed over to the sharpener and polisher the edge was tempered by a process of firing and cooling which produced the *hamon* patterns. These were given names according to their characteristics. Patterns which look as if they have been scattered with silver sand are called *nie* (bubbles), while finely scattered grains indistinguishable to the naked eye and giving a misty effect are called *nioi* (fragrance). Depending on the swordsmith or the school

either is emphasized, but usually both appear, the *nie* overlaying the finer *nioi*.

Hidehira – Geometric or gold motifs on red or black lacquer. Hidehira lacquer originated in north-eastern Japan and takes its name from Fujiwara Hidehira (1093–1187) who greatly appreciated the style.

Hira-maki-e ('flat *maki-e*') – This is the simplest *maki-e* technique for decorating lacquer. Here the design is transferred from paper and painted on to the surface of the lacquer. Metal powder is sprinkled on while the lacquer is still wet. When dry a protective coat of clear lacquer is applied and polished.

Honkozane – *Ōyoroi* (great armour) was made of leather and iron lames bound together to form horizontal tiers. The lamellar tiers are covered with lacquer and laced together vertically with thick silk lacing to create large sections, which are then joined with smaller solid iron or leather parts, *honkozane*. Metal was used if the *honkozane* were in a vulnerable part of the armour. They were all lacquered, and then painted with rust lacquer followed by a layer of black lacquer.

Inen Seal – A seal which was used by the Sōtatsu school. Inen was the pen-name of Sōtatsu; it could also be the name of the studio. The inen seal was red and round. Many kinds of seals were used by Sōtatsu and the artists of the Sōtatsu school, and there are many pictures that are only stamped, with no signature. Among these there are many which were said to have been drawn by Sōtatsu.

Inrō – Literally 'seal caddy'. Originally a container to store and protect seals. Later they developed into miniature medicine containers worn suspended from waist sashes during the Edo period.

Jō – A *Nō* play mask depicting the sacred spirit of an elderly man. Originally it represented a god but was later used to personify the spirit of a typical elderly person who had passed away.

Jūbako – Box-shaped, stacking containers for food. Many were lacquered and inlaid with mother-of-pearl.

Jutte – A defensive weapon with a large iron hook near the grip to fend off enemy swords. During the civil wars the *jutte* was about 90cm long, and was called an *uchiharai jutte*. In the Edo period, policemen carried *jutte* which were about 40cm long, with tassels attached to the grip. The tassel colour, such as purple, red and black, distinguished the policeman's rank.

Kabuki – Spectacular, popular drama of the Edo period, dealing with domestic and historical themes. Originally women took part but they were banned in 1629 as they were thought to endanger morality. In contrast to *Nō*, amazing grimaces and facial expressions were used rather than masks.

Kabuto (helmet) – Part of the protective equipment used by military commanders in battle. The helmet bowl is the *hachi*; the section hanging at the back of the *hachi*, the *shikoro*, was to protect the neck. There are helmets with the shape of gods, Buddha, animals and plants.

Kakemono – Vertical hanging scroll for painting or calligraphy.

Kamigata Ukiyo-e – *Kamigata*-pictures (the *Kyoto-Osaka* area pictures). Also called *Naniwa* woodblock prints, after the Bunka-bunsei period. The style was influenced by the Edo woodblock prints, resulting in the popularity of the prints in the Kyoto-Osaka area as well. Many of them were made using paper moulds, and the technique called *Aibazuri* for the colouring. The woodblock prints have the distinctive taste of the Kyoto-Osaka area.

Kanmuri-dai – A stand on which to place headdresses for use on Imperial ceremonial occasions.,

Kanō School – The Kanō style was based on the Chinese method of painting. It played a very important role in Japanese art, continuing until the end of the 19th century. This school of painting was founded by Kanō Masanobu, appointed painter to the Ashikaga shoguns in the latter half of the Muramachi period. He combined an authentic use of Chinese style with a free interpretation of traditional Japanese subject-matter which pointed the way forward for painting in Japan. His follower Kanō Motonobu was able to maintain production through the civil strife of the period, building up the foundations of the school. His grandson Kanō Eitoku (1543–90) had a particular talent for painting flowers and birds. He attracted the admiration of men such as Toyotomi Hideyoshi who commissioned him to paint the sliding screens forming the walls at Osaka castle. After Eitoku's death in 1590 and the move of the Tokugawa shogunate to Edo at the beginning of the next century Kanō artists set up schools in both Edo and Kyoto. Kanō Tsuenobu (1636–1713) worked in Edo. (Nos 3, 7, 12, 15, 19, 20, 21)

Katana (sword) – The Japanese method of making swords is unique. Blades were often handed down from earlier periods and presented as gifts. The signature of the swordsmith and the date, seal and name of the person to whom the sword was dedicated were inscribed on the hilt. The decoration of swords employed the skills of lacquer and metal workers.
The *daishō* ('large and small') is a pair of swords, one 60-90cm in length (*katana*), the other 30-60cm (*wakizashi*). The inscription was always placed on the side facing outwards. The pair of swords was standard for samurai from the 16th century and was worn thrust into the sash with the cutting edge facing upwards. The *daishō* had a range of metal fittings and accessories including the scabbard, which protected the sword blade and the wearer.

Kōetsu style – Styles influenced by the work of the Kōetsu family who were distinguished in several branches of the fine and decorative arts, including lacquer ware.

Kogai – An implement with an untempered blade, thought to have been for arranging the hair under the helmet. It fitted against the scabbard of a sword on the side away from the wearer.

Kogatana – A small knife inserted into a slot on the scabbard, next to the wearer's body.

TACHI

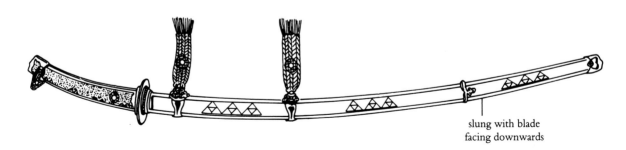

slung with blade
facing downwards

MOUNTED KATANA

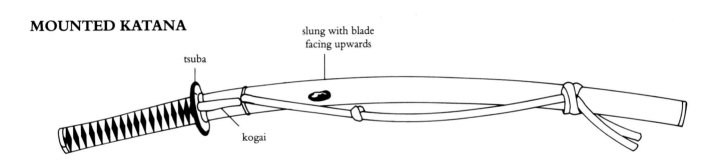

slung with blade
facing upwards

tsuba

kogai

KATANA BLADE

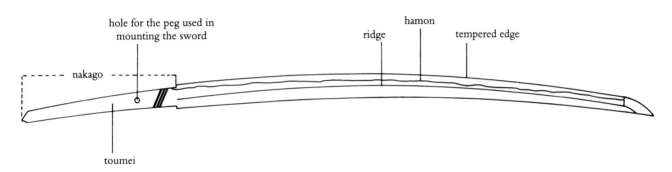

hole for the peg used in
mounting the sword

hamon

ridge

tempered edge

nakago

toumei

Kozuka – Handle of the *Kogatana*.

Kura – A saddle, made from leather or wood and used for horses or oxen. The saddle could be used to carry either people or objects. From the late Heian to the Kamakura period *Gunjin-kura* military saddles were produced, which were strong and firm for use in combat.

Kyogen – A comic theatrical interlude, originating in the 14th century and performed as part of a *Nō* play. It featured satirical or humorous dialogue.

Kyogen-men – The mask used in *Kyogen*. The *Kyogen-men* can be roughly divided into ten categories: *Buaku* (a demon); *Bishamon*, *Ebisu*, *Daikoku* and *Fukunokami* (gods of fortune); *Noborihige* (Shinto deity); *Hikihana* (male ghost); *Ōji* (old man); *Usobuki* and *Kentoku* (symbolizing the souls of animals and plants).
The masks are larger than life. Deliberately distorted and ambiguous, they are designed to make the audience laugh.

Maki-e ('sprinkled picture') – A technique for decorating lacquer. The main types are *hira-maki-e*, *taka-maki-e* and *togidashi-maki-e*. Metal dust, usually gold or silver of powdered colour, is applied to a ground built up from many coats of lacquer which are polished when dry.

Men-bako – A box for storing a mask. Such masks were worn during sacred (Shinto) songs and dances, *Nō* plays and other classical stage productions.

Mt Yoshino – The name of the northern part of the Ōmine mountain range in the north-western part of the Nara prefecture, featuring many of the historical and legendary localities of the Minamoto no Yoshitsune and the Southern Dynasty. Traditionally a famous spot for cherry blossom, and the mountain that first attracted enthusiasts of mountain climbing and ascetics. The first poem written about the cherry blossom at Yoshino was published in the *Collection of Old and New Poems*. Snowy mountains were also a favourite subject of poetry. The area is now the *Yoshino Kumano National Park*.

Nakago – The sword handle which, by its shape and the placing of the tang, could indicate maker and period. A handle used as made was called an *ubu-nakago*, while a shortened handle was a *suriage-nakago*.

Namban – 'Southern Barbarian'. The term is applied to artefacts made under European influence or for Europeans who came to Japan in the 16th and 17th centuries.

Nashiji ('Pear Skin') – A technique for decorating lacquer in which irregularly shaped flakes of metal are mixed with clear lacquer. When polished down, the sparkling, stippled effect is reminiscent of a Japanese pear. Originating in the *Kamakura* period, the technique was widely used in many variations in subsequent periods.

Negoro – Monochrome red lacquer is usually referred to as *Negoro*. The term originated from the fact that up until the Muromachi period the Negoro Temple and surrounding area in Kishū, present-day Wakayama prefecture, produced red lacquer cups and trays.

Netsuke – Traditional Japanese garments had no pockets. Small objects were carried attached by a cord through the sash around the waist. Netsuke were toggles used to counter-weight the object and stop it slipping through. Besides their practical function they became a distinct branch of the sculptor's art during the Edo period, responding to the demand of customers with money for luxury items. The main materials were wood, ivory and lacquer. Carvers drew inspiration for their subjects from all aspects of life, mythology and history, working with originality and skill.

Nihon-ga (Japanese Painting) – The subject matter, format, media and pictorial conventions of Japanese painting all derive ultimately from Chinese sources. However, these influences were incorporated and developed into many unique forms of Japanese art in each period. *Yamato-e* ('Japanese painting') originated in the 12th century and has come to be regarded as traditional Japanese painting. However, ink painting was influenced by Buddhism. The main subjects for all schools of painting were landscape and natural history. Although their work was based on the traditional *Yamato-e* it was developed by Japanese artists such as Korin and Sōtatsu into a much brighter and more colourful style based on direct observation of nature. During the Edo period the *Ukiyo-e* School brought the human figure into greater prominence through the interest of the leisurely urban classes of merchants and Samurai. The format for these works was the vertical hanging scroll (*Kake-mono*) and the horizontal handscroll (*Makimono*), which could be rolled for storage. During the 16th century larger formats developed such as sliding doors (*Fusuma*) and folding screens

(*Byobu*), which were used as room dividers. During the 16th century the Kanō School began to flourish by combining the Chinese and the *Yamato-e* styles. The success of the Kanō led to the decline of the Tosa School. The Kanō School became the main influence in Japanese painting up until the 19th century.

Nō – The classical form of Japanese theatre, originating in the 14th century and patronized by the aristocracy. It dealt with heroic themes and used spectacular costumes and masks. A wide variety of masks was used. They were small and light, made from thin wood and constructed so that the angle and the play of light could be used to express subtle shades of emotion such as anger, joy or grief. The masks are classified into five general characters: *Okina* (old holy man), *Oni* (ogre), *Jō* (a god disguised as an old man), *Onna* (woman) and *Otoko* (man).

Obi-bako – Box in which an *obi* (waist sash) was stored.

Oguri Kozukenosuke (1827–68) – A retainer of the Shogunate government in the last years of the Edo period, in 1860 he visited the United States as a government envoy. Later, he successively held various government posts and did a great deal to modernize the Shogunate government. Unable to agree with Tokugawa Yoshinobu, he resigned. Later he was arrested and executed by the new government.

Ojime – The bead used to tighten the cords holding together a series of small objects, such as the compartments of *inrō*.

Rimpa School – Rimpa was a representative school of the Edo period, noted for its refined decorative style based on *Yamato-e* originals, Japanese style painting, and allied to the Tosa school. The school was founded by Tawaraya Sōtatsu. It takes its name from the last syllable of the name Ogata Korin (1658–1716) who was one of the most influential artists working in the style. Sakai Hōitsu (1716–1829) and his pupil Susuki Kiitsu (1796–1858) were the last artists associated directly with the school. The decorative beauty of the Rimpa style greatly influences Japanese design in painting, lacquerware, dyeing and porcelain decoration even today. (Nos 5, 6, 13, 22, 23)

Sage-jū – *Sage-ju* was used for outdoor feasts such as flower viewing and picnics. It consisted of a portable tier of boxes. There were two types of *sage-jū*: in one the tier of boxes was placed on a stand and in the other there was space for rice wine bottles, cups and plates to be inserted.

Shibayama craftmanship – An ivory craft which started in the middle of the Edo period. Coral, tortoise shell and coloured ivory were inlaid into ivory; thin layers of mother-of-pearl were used in lacquer-work. The technique was studied by *Shibayama Senzō* in *Shimōsa* (in *Chiba* prefecture) during the years from 1772–81. It survived until the *Meiji* period, mainly used on export goods.

Suji-kabuto – A style of helmet in use from the 14th to the latter half of the 16th century. The crown is a series of long, thin metal plates held together with rivets, the heads of which are hammered flat. This construction was stronger than earlier styles. Sometimes up to 122 plates and 600 rivets were used. The greater the number of plates, the higher the rank of the wearer.

Sumi – Indian ink, used for drawing and calligraphy. Made from charcoal.

Suzuri-bako – A writing box containing an ink stone, a water container, a brush, knife, gimlet and *sumi*-ink. This was standardized in the Heian period. Most of the boxes were lacquered in red and decorated with other lacquer techniques and inlaid with mother-of-pearl. Many excellent lacquered writing boxes were made during the Muromachi period. After the Edo period a variety of these boxes appeared in portable or stacked form.

Tachi – A curved sword used from the latter half of the Heian period. Before then swords were straight and used with a one-handed grip for stabbing. The *tachi* was long, held with both hands, and designed for cutting. Usually the blade curved sharply into the hilt. This type of sword was popular from the 12th to the 14th century.

Taka-maki-e ('high *maki-e*') – A *maki-e* technique for decorating lacquer in which a design is built up in relief by mixing powdered charcoal or clay into the lacquer before metal dust is applied.

Tarai – Bowl for hot or cold water which was used for washing the face, hands or feet.

Tatsuta River – The source of the river is located in northern Nara to the north-west of the Mt Ikoma, and from Ikaruga it flows from west to south to join with the Yamato River. The upper stream is called the Ikoma River, the midstream the Heguri. On both sides there are many maple trees, a famous spot for autumnal foliage. A poem written by Ariwara no Narihira is well known.

Togidashi-maki-e ('polished-out *maki-e*') – A *maki-e* technique for decorating lacquer in which a design in *hira-maki-e* is covered with further layers of lacquer. Charcoal is used to polish away the layers until the design emerges flush with the background.

Tōkaidō – Coastal highway from Edo to Kyoto. There were 53 post stations along the route.

Tokugawa Ieyasu (1542–1616) – The first shogun during the Tokugawa period, Ieyasu became shogun in 1603 after his victory at the Battle of Sekigahara. He laid the foundations of the Edo government which lasted for about 270 years.

Tosa School – The Tosa school followed the style of *Yamato-e*, Japanese style painting. It has a dubious lineage dating back to the 13th century. Fujiwara Yukimitsu was artist-in-ordinary to the Imperial Palace, two generations before Mitsunobu (1434–1525) was promoted to Director of the Imperial Painting Office (Edokoro) which established the Tosa school. During the Momoyama period the style ran parallel to that of the very active Kano school. In the Edo period there were schools both in Kyoto and Edo. Areas of flat colour with detailed drawing of subjects taken from life at court, tales of medieval battles and their heroes, or natural history typify this style. (Nos 2, 8, 10, 11)

Toumei – The signature of the swordsmith is engraved in the handle. The custom of engraving signatures began in the latter half of the Heian period. Most of the signatures consisted of two characters, either decorative or the characters used by the school, rather than the swordsmith's name. A handle without a signature is called *mu-mei* (no sign). The swords tested by experts were called *kanjo-mei*. The inscription on a tested sword was called *tameshi-mei*, and a sword with a sign on the reverse was *orikaeshi-mei*.

Tsuba – A sword guard with an opening to take a blade. Its function was to protect the hand. Before the 16th century the swordsmith made the guards himself, but gradually specialist guard-makers emerged. Guards from the 16th century onwards are highly valued as *objets d'art*.

Ukiyo-e prints – Prints of the *Ukiyo-e* (floating world) school. In style they are a continuation of the *Yamato-e* tradition, based on outlines filled with flat colour. Their production was stimulated by the demand of the leisurely urban classes of merchants and Samurai. The subject matter of the prints reflects their world and interests—courtesans, tea-houses, actors and *Kabuki*, wrestlers and landscape. The cutting and printing of wood-blocks was an extremely skilled process. The design was drawn in ink, then pasted face down on to a block of prepared cherry wood. The blockmaker cut around the lines, leaving them in relief. Black and white impressions were taken from this key-block. Separate blocks were cut with the areas for each colour. Blocks were cut on both sides. The key-block was then printed in black ink by placing damp paper on top of it and rubbing the back. When dry the first colour was printed and then the others in turn. It was a hand process and did not involve a press. Colour had to be wiped on to the block with the lightness or density of the final effect required, and each colour had to be printed in exact register with the one before.

Waka – A 31 syllable poem and the major verse form up until the Edo period when it was superseded by the seventeen syllable *haiku*.

Wan – A wooden, lidded food container for soup or rice. Some are decorated with plain lacquer, while others have designs in *maki-e*.

Yutō – A lacquered utensil with a spout and handle for pouring hot water or *sake*.

Index of Artists

Acknowledgments

The National Museums of Scotland are most grateful to the staff of the Tokyo Fuji Art Museum for their contributions to this catalogue. We should particularly like to thank Tatsuo Takakura, Executive Vice-President, Mitsunari Noguchi, Chief Curator, Atsuhiro Momota, Curator and Yukihiro Omae, Curator.

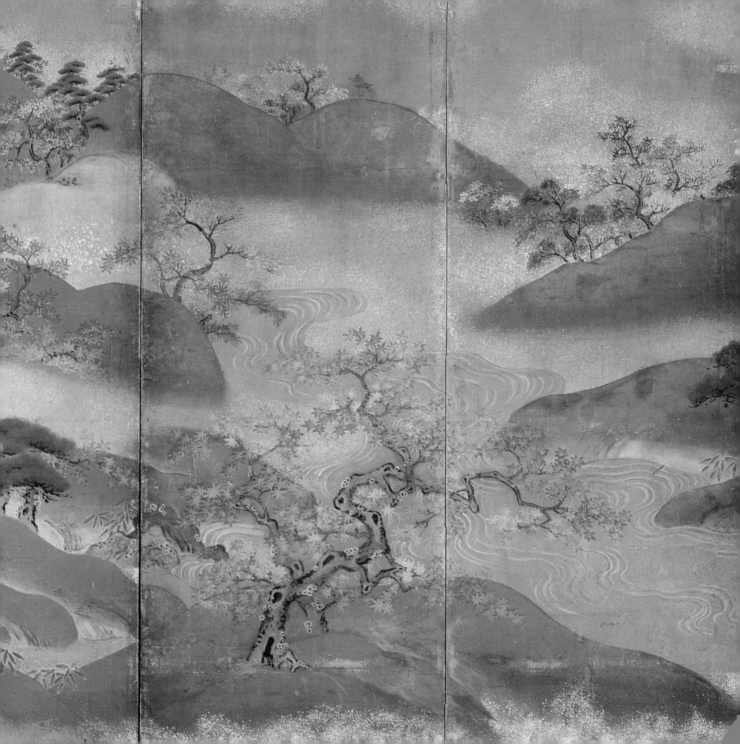